AF417565

# MY

Do you know

# LETTER

the reason your atheist

# TO THE

is your love for God?

# ATHEIST

**67** LESSONS THAT EXPLAIN **God**

## SUNDAY WILLIAM
## ELIJAH KATURAMU

My Letter To The Atheist : Do you know the reason your atheist is your love for God? 67 lessons that explain God.



Printed in United States of America



ISBN : 978-9-913-97880-4

# Acknowledgment

To all those who gathered at my mother, Madam Nsasiirwe's residence in Kyebando. As you read this book, you will understand the deep gratitude we share for God's blessings. Despite our small numbers, we worshipped with fervor and dedication to the true God. This invaluable gift to the world has come to fruition through your unwavering faith and the spiritual guidance from our communal gatherings. Your steadfast belief has been recognized by God, and through your influence, A blessed of God has emerged to illuminate the true essence of God to the world.

Special thanks to my mother, Mrs. Nsasiirwe Nantubwe Rachael; my sister, Mrs. Nuwagaba Irene Kasirye; my brother, Mr. Turinawe Michael; my friends, Ms. Mbabazi Christine, Mr. and Mrs. Nsubuga along with their son Nsubuga; Mr. Aine Collins; Mr. Musimenta Deus; Ms. Ndibalekera Rosira; Ms. Tibahwa Diana. In memory of the late Mugisha David and Pastor Irumba Lauben.

Lastly, a sincere message to my wife, Caroline Katuramu, and son, Jeremiah Christian Muhumuza. Your unwavering support, even during my silent moments, means the world to me.

When I tell you the truth, it does not matter if you do not believe me. Because the written word of truth is addressed to those who believe. When you believe, then you have met the truth. The truth is the Lord Jesus Christ, to whom I bear witness.

# Table of Contents

# PREFACE

The time has come for the world to know who the Lord God is. The Lord God is a God of all people who loves all people in this life. You were all created by God and it's because of him that you are on this earth. No one found his way on this earth without the power of God. God loves his people, and he works every day for his children to know who he is. You are the children of God created from his love. He loves you for who you are and what you are to become because of who he is. He brought you here for he knew exactly what he needed from you. You are his love and for this love, I come to you all.

I come to you all in the name of the Father, the SON, the Lord Jesus Christ. I come to you all by the power of the Holy Spirit through whom I write all you see and read in this book. This book is your encounter with the Holy Spirit. This book represents an understanding of the teachings of the Holy Spirit. This book holds the guidelines to an understanding of the scriptures as presented in the holy Bible.

For this book presents life which life opens your eyes and ears to the Lord you serve. The Lord God is a God of love who is available to all men who seek him. The Lord God whom you serve is the God I write and talk about in this book. This God is a God who wants the world to know who he is and what he is. I come to teach all man about God and the ways of God. I come to this earth to teach the world the bad ways of the world for the world to go away from sin. For sin is invisible to man for man knows less when he sins. For the devil has made sin invisible to man that man now walks with sin. For all men have decided to be in sin and forgot the righteous path. For all people on earth are fighting to go away from the righteous path in support of sin.

Sin has become part of man and now man knows no righteousness. Man has looked for sin and now man's ways are with sin. Sin has made man forget God and now God has no one to protect the world from sin. For the men in the church are scared to talk about sin. For the preachers in church fear to remind the world of sin. For sin has grown in strength. For the greatest sinners are the most powerful. For they are powerful and they control all the world needs. They are so powerful that they destroy anything that talks about their sinful lives they walk. But the Lord God created this world and nothing in this world or the Spirit will stop him from putting the world right as he desires. For it's his creation and all creations follow his rules. For this world is his creation and will follow his rules for he created it. For this world is his creation and no one goes away from his rules will have life.

The Lord God gives no life to those who go away from his word. The Lord God loves no sin for sin teaches man to be against his God. This is satan the author of sin. This is satan who is seated in the hearts of all sinful men of the world. This is satan who the world has failed to know, and he has taken the world away from the path of the Lord.

This book is a book to teach man about God and the ways of God. For I have walked this world and the world ways are not God's ways. For I come to the world to show the world who the sin is. I know the sin, and come to teach the world of the sin. The Lord God wants man to know who the sin is. The Lord wants man to learn the sin and man to understand what the sin wants. I am here to teach you all of the devil satan. lucifer the son of sin who moves in the hearts of all sinful men of the world. For the world has failed to see the sin and I come to teach you of the sin. For I know the sin and I have what the world needs to know about sin. For I know satan and satan fears the truth about him to be known to the world. For when the world knows the truth about satan, it will defeat him.

I come to the world to teach the world of who the Lord God is. For the Lord is in me and I am in Him. For HIS within me and there is nothing I say on my own behalf. For HE is within me and what I say is HIS own word. Nothing comes out of my word on my own but HE who is in me. For am not here for my own good but to accomplish that which HE has sent me.

This word is a word of the Holy Spirit. This word is the power of the Holy Spirit  who sends it to the world to open the eyes of all man. This word is the word of the Father the Lord Jesus Christ. For the Spirit of the Lord testifies on his behalf. This word is the word of good news to all those who believe in the Lord Jesus Christ. For no man present in this world was there when the scriptures were written. For no man present was there to meet any of the writers of the scriptures. For many men have failed to worship God for they don't know who their God is. How special are you who have believed in the word of God and still follow his commands? For the kingdom of God is yours. How grateful is it for the Lord to come to his servants in this world? For the world will know who he is and the world will understand who its creator is. How lucky are you men of this generation for the Lord has come to you, to teach you of the ways of your God? How lucky are you men of this generation who will die knowing who their God is?

That Your Way May Be Known On The Earth,
Your Salvation Among All Nations.

# INTRODUCTION

God's message is meant for all the earth's inhabitants, regardless of their beliefs. Every individual is a creation of God, and God intentions are inherently kind towards His creations. Misunderstandings have obscured the true nature of God, leading to widespread confusion. From ancient times, the devil has misled man, steering him away from God's path. Many are unaware of the genuine God, as the devil has craftily taken on a God like role in the world. Recognizing the unique existence of God is crucial; those who honor beings other than the true God are considered non-believers, often labeled as Atheists. Material wealth, women, money, and modern technology have unintentionally become idols, diminishing the worship due to God. This is similar to the reverence for buddha, engaging in voodoo, or following islam, none of which represent the one true God. God is one, striving to reveal His true self to mankind. Unfortunately, the majority have struggled to understand the true essence of the Almighty.

When I speak of the one true God, I refer to the God of Israel. This is the God who, across many generations, has waged wars for His people, so they may know Him and follow His ways. He sacrificed men and nations for the sake of one individual's enlightenment. To individually know Him is to be like the mustard seed—small and solitary when sown, yet it grows into a vast tree with broad branches that shelter animals and nest birds. To know Him is to emulate the Lord Jesus Christ, a solitary seed planted in the earth that, through its death, yielded innumerable seeds to broaden the kingdom of God. God's love extends to all man, but satan, through deception, has persuaded many that God is nonexistent. He fostered sin through wickedness and has now infiltrated the church to destroy what he believes is left of God.

I write to you because no one would rise and choose to worship what they do not believe to be God. No Muslim believes their worship is directed at anything but God, nor do buddhists, nor the Indians who follow krishna and others. They all believe they are worshipping the true God. This book guides you to a precise understanding of who God is. Understanding God goes beyond reading and acknowledging; it involves drawing in his presence. This book outlines methods to invoke God and feel his presence. It is a well-crafted guide for all people on earth who doubt God's existence, to help them find their way. It provides clear instructions that, when followed, allow you to experience the God of Israel.

I hold love for all man and yearn for everyone to discover the truth about their God. The truth is accessible and proclaimed openly, yet many do not heed because they search for God in grandeur. It is through simplicity that God moves, and the straightforward words in this book will enlighten you to the true God we worship.

**Sunday William Elijah Katuramu**

# MY LETTER TO THE ATHEIST

# Lesson One

# GOD IS THE WHOLE DESCRIPTION OF LOVE

Apostle Paul's portrayal of love in the scriptures reflects the love of the Lord God. By articulating these sentiments, Paul is portraying God Himself. Those who aspire to embody the love Paul depicts in the scriptures should look to the Lord their God. Indeed, he represents the love that Paul articulates.

The boundless love of the Lord, our divine Creator, is unmatched by any man. God's love is the ultimate expression of compassion and grace, unparalleled by any earthly or heavenly being. It is this love that inspired Him to create mankind with exquisite magnificence. In His eyes, humanity is the crowning glory of His creations, imbued with true beauty. Therefore, humanity stands as a  living tribute to love, echoing the divine love of the Lord God within them.

In the scriptures, Paul imparts to man the true essence of love, stating that love is patient and kind. It does not envy or boast, and it is not arrogant. It does not dishonor others, nor is it self-centered or quick to anger; it keeps no tally of wrongs. Love takes no pleasure in wrongdoing but celebrates the truth. It consistently protects, trusts, hopes, and endures.

# PAUL'S PORTRAYAL OF LOVE IS AN ACCURATE DEPICTION OF GOD THE FATHER.

For God is patient, and God is kind. God does not envy, God does not boast, and God is not proud. God does not dishonor others, God is not self-seeking, God is not easily angered, and God keeps no record of wrongs. God does not delight in evil but rejoices with the truth. God protects, trusts, gives hope, and always perseveres.

The love of man towards his fellow man should mirror that of  his

Creator. We are called to love one another as the Lord, our God, loves us. His love is unconditional, not based on our deeds but present even before our existence was known. Yet, humans often judge and harbor hatred for one another's sins. Remember, no one is born sinful.

God's love was so profound that He sent His son to atone for our sins. When God gazes upon humanity, He sees the love with which He created us, which love He desires in heaven.

How can we join God in heaven if we fail to emulate His character? Let every person reflect God's love in everything they do. Not the worldly love, but that of our Creator. For When you harbor hatred for one another due to your sinful nature, you undermine the salvation available to all mankind.

# Lesson Two

# THE BEST COMMANDMENT

When you have love for God, His goodness comes along. This goodness empowers individuals to withstand temptations. A person who has God within them will not violate His commandments.

# LOVE THE LORD YOUR GOD WITH ALL YOUR HEART, ALL YOUR SOUL, AND ALL YOUR MIND.' THIS IS THE FIRST AND MOST IMPORTANT COMMAND.

God is the origin of life, and everything exists because of God. Love and hate stem from God, as He is the creator of all. The Lord God, who created everything, has the deepest understanding of love and hate. When God advises us to avoid sin, His knowledge of sin surpasses human perception.

Sin stands as the opposite of God, serving as the force that distances man from God. Sin is the destruction of the heavens and sin is the destruction of salvation. When you hate God, you hate all that is good. When hate comes deep into your heart, you will fail with God. For the fruits of the devil multiply on grounds that rebel against God.

The Lord Jesus Christ commanded you man to Love the Lord your God with all your heart, all your soul, and all your mind. This is the first and most important command. For when you love God, you call all his goodness to yourself. When you love God, you bring closer the true love which love will fail all the darkness that fights man.

I teach that all the Ten Commandments, as given to Moses, are encompassed by this commandment: to love the Lord, your God, with all your heart, soul, and mind. When you do so, you will not place any Gods before the Almighty, create idols for worship, take the Lord's name in vain, or fail to keep the Sabbath holy. You will honor your parents, not commit murder, adultery, theft, or bear false witness against your neighbor, and you will not covet. For the Lord your God resides within you, and what comes out from you reflects the God in your heart.

# Lesson Three

# THE WAR
# YOU DO NOT SEE

Human beings often believe they are independent and solely responsible for their decisions. However, our lives are shaped by forces that surpass our comprehension. Failing to grasp these powers leads to a lack of understanding on how to lead a virtuous life in the presence God.

We trust that everything is as God intended, and we are unable to alter it. By doing so, we leave ourselves vulnerable to the devil, resulting in ongoing setbacks. God created the world according to His plan. However, it is essential for Man to recognize the adversaries of God that have caused human failures. As it's written, "For we wrestle not against flesh and blood, but against principalities, against powers, against the rulers of the darkness of this world." You should realize as a follower of Christ; many of the events in your lives are a manifestation of the spiritual world.

## NINETY PERCENT OF YOUR WORDS AND ACTIONS ARE NOT ENTIRELY YOUR OWN, BUT RATHER THE RESULT OF INFLUENCES.

You stand against adversaries intent on justifying their wrongful cause. This willing devil employs his might to thwart those who worship the Lord God. Once basking in God's presence and aware of His glory, he chose rebellion driven by selfish aims. His desire is for all to emulate him, making you his foe when you invoke the name of the Lord Jesus Christ. Your existence is evidence of these spirits' transgressions. They were angels, endowed with greater wisdom than humans, yet you have achieved what they refused: to worship the Lord your God as he truly is.

This is a hidden battle that demands your attention and concern. The devil is determined to see you stumble. These malevolent forces are always active, ceaselessly working to bring harm to all, regardless of their beliefs. Whether you follow Christ or not, the devil harbors no goodwill towards humanity. The arrival of the Lord Jesus Christ on earth designated man as a substitute for the devil. As it is stated, "They are not of the world, just as I am not of the world." The devil will engage in a continuous battle and attempt to influence your decisions every moment. To resist the devil's negative influence, it is essential to pray, worship, and invite the presence of the Lord into your life consistently.

# Lesson Four

# OUR FATHER,
# WHICH ART IN HEAVEN

The prayer that the Lord Jesus Christ taught mankind
(Our Father, In Heaven) is a powerful tool to connect
with Him in heaven. By understanding and utilizing
this prayer, individuals can combat the evils in their
surroundings. It encompasses everything necessary to
capture the divine attention of God.

You show little interest in the Lord's Prayer, sometimes over looking its significance and power in overcoming challenges. In church, you recite it casually, as if it were just another old song.

This prayer, taught by God Himself, enables you to reach Him. It removes any obstacles in your path as you seek the Father in heaven. Truly, when you recite the Lord's Prayer, you have prayed. Whether it takes one minute or less, your prayer is heard, and the Lord listens. This prayer encompasses all your needs and essentials for worship. Using the words provided by the Lord, this prayer can be used to address all other concerns in your life.

## THIS IS HOW YOU PRAY WITHIN THE LORD'S PRAYER.

*Our Father, who art in heaven, hallowed be thy name; thy kingdom come; thy will be done on earth as it is in heaven.*

Our Father, whose glory is manifested in both the earth and the heavens, may your name be glorified. For you have done well to everyone and showed mercy to the innocent. For your righteousness and love for truth, you dwell in the heavens with the righteous. You love no evil and for that reason, you cast out the devil from your presence. My Lord, that same devil has come to destroy me. He has stood ahead of my prosperity and hindered my righteousness so that I see light no more. As you cast him out of the heavens, cast him out of my life. Cast him out of my job, my marriage, my children, and my walk with you. This way, through me, your will to be done on this earth and I follow your commands as set forth.

## Give us this day our daily bread; and forgive us our trespasses as we forgive those who trespass against us;

Heavenly Father, as you fed the Israelites in the wilderness with manna, and they never went hungry.  As you daily feed the birds in the air, feed your servant with your daily bread. This bread is your body and blood. This bread is your word, Lord Jesus Christ. Let me wake up daily with your word to lead me through the day. Let your word strengthen me to move on amidst the darkness that surrounds this earth. My father, as I ask for forgiveness, I repent of all my sins. Those I have known and those I know less. Sins of my fathers and grandfathers. May I through your forgiveness Lord, gain the strength to forgive all those who have wronged me. For no man can forgive unless it's by your grace.

## Lead us not into temptation but deliver us from evil. For the kingdom, the power, and the glory are yours now and forever. Amen.

Heavenly Father, Your involvement in no evil is evident through Your works since the beginning of human understanding. My Father, You are aware of the evil one and his evil ways towards Your creation. Heavenly

Father, shield me from his path. Remind me daily of Your presence and love, as You did for those You cherished before me, that I may walk in Your truth and righteousness. For all glory on earth and in heaven belongs to You, now and forever, Amen.

# Lesson Five

# THE LORD
# IS MY SHEPHERD

Humans can connect with God through His word, as it
serves as a covenant between them and God. Whatever a
person requests through God's word,
God will attentively hear.

There has been a shift in the church's focus on what is significant to the Lord and how to approach God. Nowadays, more emphasis is placed on the New Testament while the Old Testament is sometimes overlooked. It's crucial to remember that the Old Testament holds the origins of all  written scriptures and shapes humanity's perception of God. The teachings from the Old Testament are reflected in the words of the Lord Jesus Christ. Every word written is connected to Him, including those spoken through David. When reciting powerful prayers like David's Psalm "The Lord Is My Shepherd," approach them with reverence and understanding. These scriptures are special prayers that should not be missed before bedtime, as they hold deep meaning and provide direct communication with the Lord.

Engaging in the act of writing God's word or serving the Lord is often accompanied by great temptations, as the devil's battles persist. It is through the Holy Spirit that one is able to write at all, even if it is merely reciting the Psalms. In doing so, one may feel resistance, as the devil strives to prevent the recitation of these Psalms. This understanding sheds light on the struggles faced by the prophets and King David in penning God's word, as preserved in the Holy Scriptures. These efforts should not be in vain, for these words represent God's salvation and His promises to all mankind. The words of David's Psalm, "The Lord Is My Shepherd, have those words to strengthen and give hope to all man who rightly use them.

No one truly knows how to pray, as you are uncertain what stands before you. Many often pray about what they perceive as the problem, which may not be the actual issue. Instead of offering thanks or praying in repentance, they immediately lament their troubles. However, one can pray to God through David's Psalms, 'The Lord Is My Shepherd,' in the manner as guided with the Lord's Prayer in Lesson Four. This approach brings forth God's promises as revealed in the Psalms of David.

# WHO ARE YOU IN DAVID'S PSALMS "THE LORD IS MY SHEPHERD'?

*The Lord is your saviour, and you need no one besides him. He gives you peace and protects you through his love. Like the green pastures with no stones, snakes, or thorns, His love is different from what the world gives. With His love, He protects you from evil and fills your heart with the joy of his love. He feels your heart with his commands that you never go out of his way. Even through your times of trial, you will resist all temptations. For you know God is with you and for his name, he can never leave you to destruction. The Lord lifts you over your enemies. He gives you the child you have been looking for, He builds your life so that your enemies will serve you and kneel on your feet. The Lord showers you with blessings far beyond what the world expects, and his love and mercy will follow you in all walks of your life. He will be your tang when you speak. He will shield you and create fear within your enemies. His love will be seen through you for the glory of his name. You will be his child, and he will be your father for eternity.*

## THE PSALM OF DAVID, PSALMS 23 IS THE TRUE TEACHING FROM DAVID OF THE LIFE OF A MAN WHO WALK IN THE FULLNESS OF THE HOLY SPIRIT. HIS WORDS PAINT A TRUE IMAGE OF A MAN FILLED WITH THE HOLY SPIRIT.

# Lesson Six

# "LIFE"
# IS A GAIN THROUGH DEATH

Our purpose on this earth is not solely for earthly pleasures but to strive towards the afterlife. It is essential for individuals to realize that our actions here are aimed at attaining the riches of heaven.  For the kingdom of heaven is like a man, who sells all his possessions to purchase that single treasure, he found.

Life can be a challenge and a struggle to find a true meaning. This life is like a man, who hears about God and cares less about what he hears. It could be these Muslim brothers, who are daily attacking those who praise and worship the Lord God and try to silence them. They don't consider Jesus as God.  Since childhood, have been blinded to the truth about the God of Israel. But one day, they will say to themselves, let me try the Jesus they keep talking about. They will go on their knees and say "my God and my Lord Jesus Christ, I am in your presence, after failing where I have been. I humble myself before you. So that when I pray, you come to me".

Life is valued through the gains of the life after death. The beauty of this life is how you realize this life is for nothing. You realize all you have left in this life is to run to God with much joy and hope in the life he gives after death. Am talking about the beauty of that moment when God's Angels bring you forward to the Lord Jesus Christ after winning the earthly battles.

One should always commit themselves to the Lord Jesus Christ. Looking through life, one may realize it's all in vain without God. Life only finds true meaning through the Lord God. One should never cease to speak of sin. Sin, once recognized, should be rebuked, whether within the church or outside. Church pews are often filled with men in sin, yet there is a reluctance to address sin. Consider a man, well-known in his church, who appeared on the 10 o'clock news for attempting to seize land from squatters and threatening to demolish their homes. That

Sunday, he attended church, was seated at the front during a fundraiser, and contributed the largest sum. The congregation was pleased, but did he acknowledge his wrongdoing? He did not. While I may condemn his actions, I hold the church accountable for honoring his faults. Respecting unholy weaknesses in people is a sin. This sin leads them to hell. God, through His prophet, is explicit about this sin and its judgment, stating, "O wicked man, you will surely die," and if one does not persuade him to change his ways, that wicked man will die for his sin, and the silent observer will be held responsible. However, if you do warn the wicked to turn from his ways and he does not, he will die for his sin, but you will have saved yourself.

The message of the Lord's prophet did not cease; rather, throughout history, God has sent holy men to remind humanity of its sins. The Lord himself descended to this world and is present on this earth to demonstrate the nature of sin. Thus, no one can claim that God remains silent about sin. Similarly, it is incumbent upon man to speak candidly about sin, to safeguard his soul.

Lesson Seven

# LET THE SINNERS KNOW THEY SIN

Are you afraid to tell sinners of their sins? Is it because you fear hatred? By failing to acknowledge their sins, you respect and maintain their sinfulness, thus becoming a sinner yourself.

The world is gripped by a fear that has diverted it from the truth. Such is the fear of one's fellow man that some would rather risk going to Hell than offend another's pride. There is a hesitation to confront the wrongdoings of leaders, and a reluctance to speak the truth to those in power who cause harm and death to the innocent. Moreover, God's Bishops and priests, seated in high authority, are often the first to praise these evildoers. Church leaders have been seduced into supporting politicians whose hearts resonate with worldly desires, not with God. But the Scriptures warn that failing to rebuke the sinner is to share in their sin, for witnessing injustice and remaining silent you partake in their sin.

"In Africa, people see a young girl in a relationship with a man they all know is sick with **AIDS**, they keep silent. You're not different from the man intentionally sleeping with this young girl to make her sick."

"A certain woman who was infected with **AIDS** got into a relationship with a young boy. Every single day, neighbours in her compound, who knew she was infected with **AIDS**, saw her with this young boy and said nothing. After the boy was infected with **AIDS**, he narrated his story. He recalled everyone he met and interacted with during his relationship with this woman, including the friend who convinced him to pursue a relationship with her. The grandmother, who aware of the woman's illness, could only inquire about the boy's relationship with her. He recalls the words of the woman after infecting him with **AIDS**, "I too was infected by someone, find one else to spread it to. "All these have unknowingly committed the same sin, spreading AIDS to the innocent boy." Sinners must be aware of their sins. This is the reason the Lord Jesus Christ came and is on this earth, saying, "I have come so that the blind will see." I do not partake in unrighteousness and do not contradict my word. On the cross, I opened your eyes to recognize sin. You have learned to identify and combat sin. Who among you can accuse me concerning my word?

Your eyes have been opened to recognize sin. This gift is meant for you to help others see their own sins. Ultimately, every person should have the ability to identify sin and possess the strength to oppose it. I write to remind you of the Lord's mission in granting you this vision. For with the coming of light into the world, sin can no longer hide itself.

## Lesson Eight

# "GOD" IS MAN'S ONLY LENS TO THE FUTURE

We journey through life believing we understand all there is to know, yet we harbor fear for the unknown of tomorrow. We strive for material possessions, uncertain if time will allow us to enjoy them. The certainty of our presence tomorrow remains elusive. For those with faith, God is the sole window into the future.

There is a time when particular moments have a stronger meaning and when such moments will have the strongest relevance. A man was admitted to a mental hospital. In these wards, it was he and another patient William admitted in ward number 22. In these wards, he felt lonely, for he knew less what was next in his life.

In this earthly walk, though you are with someone, life will always be lonely. This is especially true if your strength is with this world. All that happens is a struggle within yourself that not even you can understand. It is only the Father who sets it to be who understands it all.

With a hymn book in his hands, all he could afford was to sing and call upon the Lord his God. He recalls this moment as the only time he meaningfully sang and worshipped the Lord God. For this was the moment the Lord God opened up his mind to who he truly was in this world.

You can never know what is next in your life apart from the father who set it to be. Only Hymns and written scriptures will be your companions to give meaning to the life you live. You will be neglected and abused by all those you trust.

For no one knows how their life will end on this earth. All you see and understand is what your eyes can look at. You don't see far beyond your present to avoid the circumstances in the future of your life. For it's not in your creation to see far beyond what you know. Life becomes a risk to all of you who walk on this earth. For you do all things pretending there is hope in tomorrow, but you see no tomorrow.

The Lord God is the only lens to the future. He gives hope to those who believe in him. His hope is not what you want to see on this earth but his hope is what you're after in this life. This life is a path to the next world with the Father. Only those who have the lens can see the future and have hope in life. Only those who are with Christ have hope for the future and can manage to live humble lives. For they don't struggle for this world. For they know the greatest gift exists and that gift is what the Lord Jesus gives to man after death. This gift is the life everlasting that God has set for all those who believe in him. This life is set for all who believe in him on this earth and those he guides to the day of their death. Death is no threat to men of God for they await that day to join with the Father and see the greatness of their God. That is a lens far more divine than what the eyes of man can see. This lens comes to only those who believe and give their lives to the Lord Jesus Christ.

That lens is the Holy Spirit. He has come and is present to all men who believe in him. For those who believe in him, he guides. Through his gifts, he opens their eyes to the world far beyond their imaginations. To those who believe in his power, he protects them from evil until the time when he leads them to heaven. I am the spirit of the Lord, and all those who believe in me I will guide and lead them to the righteous path of the Lord Jesus Christ. Those who hear and keep my word will win the battles of this world, and I will lead them to the Lord Jesus Christ. For I come to the world to do that I was sent to do. For I come to the world to give comfort to all man in the name of the Lord Jesus Christ. For I come to the world to protect and guide all man that has built his trust in the Lord Jesus Christ. For I am the power of the world, through my power and through the name of the Lord Jesus Christ, man will reach the Father.

## Lesson Nine

# WE HAVE MADE SIN A FRIEND

**Man has become so accustomed to sin that man often does not recognize when he sins. What was once deemed sinful is now accepted as normal due to man's sinful nature. This disconnect has led to a failure to understand God, allowing sin to proliferate freely among God's people.**

Belief in the Lord Jesus Christ signifies engagement in a spiritual battle. This battle involves following the righteous path to the Father in Heaven. It is not a battle fought alone in this earthly life, but alongside other forces in the spiritual world. This journey is among the most challenging ones to undertake. It is important to recognize that not everyone who believes in the Lord Jesus Christ as God knows precisely how to reach Him. The scriptures are there to guide you on this path, yet comprehension of these scriptures requires the guidance of the Holy Spirit .

Discovering the Holy Spirit  and, through His grace, uncovering the hidden meanings within the scriptures transforms you into a true soldier. This is the soldier that Paul describes, one who engages not only in earthly battles but also combats the fallen angels. Such battles are not for the spiritually immature, the breastfeeding, as the scriptures say, but for those who have attained a profound understanding of the spiritual world. In discussing spiritual growth, I echo the words of my Lord, Christ Jesus, about me, the Holy Spirit. My purpose is to foster your spiritual growth. This maturation unveils aspects of satan and realities of God that have never been acknowledged by the world. The enemy operates within the spiritual world, subtly influencing your actions without revealing his presence.  This is why he is referred to as operating in the dark.

The thief arrives in the night, under the cover of darkness, when everyone is asleep, and all lights are off. Despite going unnoticed, the thief's actions cause harm to many, embodying evil, and that is the devil. The devil's influence has normalized unholy behaviors, leading people to associate themselves with evil. Terms like cross-gender, natural gays, and lesbians are used, even extending to openly acknowledging being natural liars. By embracing the devil, the master of hate, you have unknowingly welcomed darkness into your lives. To comprehend this darkness, it is crucial to welcome the Holy Spirit and His mercy. Those who follow God's path can discern the signs of darkness, for he gives them the grace to see and understand its presence.

As I sit in this office, the devil is singing a well-known American pop song. Within seconds, an employee in the same office starts singing the same song in the same rhythm, immediately, the devil stops singing. Why do I share this with you, why reveal such profound truth? To demonstrate that humanity needs God. To illustrate that our minds and decisions are influenced, and we have no control over what we hear, say, or think. Even the choice of your spouse is not truly your own. The spiritual world governs this earth in every aspect. The only variance is who governs over you. According to the Book of Revelation, a third of the angels fell, becoming devils. But what constitutes a third of heaven? It could be 10 million, a billion, or perhaps twice the population of Earth's existence. A third represents roughly 33% of the angels, far more than one might assume. The Lord Jesus Christ states in the scriptures, "When an unclean spirit leaves a person, it takes seven other spirits more wicked than itself along." There are more evil spirits than what mankind believes.

Remain steadfast and battle for the Lord's glory. Stand resolute and strive to lead a life that the Lord requires. But how does one lead such a life without comprehending the darkness? Understanding the dark is not achieved solely through theological education that imparts scripture and worldly knowledge. The Pharisees and scribes were the most avid readers of scripture, which was their law and guide for living. However, their understanding of God was minimal. You may read everything I have written in these scriptures and still have questions, for their understanding will fail you. But there is a sovereign over the world—God himself, the Holy Spirit , whose delight is in enlightening you about the enemy, rejoicing when man stands valiantly against the darkness. Embrace the Lord, and all this and more will be revealed to you. Darkness may be invisible and seem formidable, but it is weak. Have faith in the Lord, and you will realize the power He can bestow upon you.

# Lesson Ten

# THE GIFTS OF
# THE HOLY SPIRIT

**Exercise caution in labeling someone as 'gifted,' for numerous false prophets exist. When you hear an individual speaking in tongues, how can you discern if it is genuine tongues being spoken?**

As the Lord Jesus Christ was ascending to heaven, He promised you an advocate. The scriptures record: "But the Advocate, the Holy Spirit , whom the Father will send in my name, will teach you all things and remind you of everything I have said to you."

The Lord Jesus Christ has entrusted you to the care of the Holy Spirit . You Surrender yourselves to the Holy Spirit . As Paul taught, "the Holy Spirit  assists us in our weaknesses. We may not know what we should pray for, but the Spirit itself intercedes on our behalf with unspoken groanings."

The subject of the Holy Spirit is profoundly complex, and this complexity intensifies when discussing His gifts. These gifts have significantly perplexed the church. A renowned preacher described the gift of the Holy Spirit  (speaking in tongues) to his congregation, saying, "When I am free or sad, I go to my room, lock myself in, and speak in tongues." Did this preacher comprehend his own words? Another pastor claimed, "I prayed for my church congregation, and everyone began speaking in tongues." However, the scriptures teach through Paul that when you speak in tongues, someone must interpret them. The real question is, has anyone ever encountered an interpreter of tongues? It's not that Paul's teachings are incorrect, but rather that many have misinterpreted his words. Paul's instruction that tongues should have an interpreter means that there must be an interpretation when one speaks in tongues.

Tongues and other spiritual gifts come from the Holy Spirit. You receive God's abilities without becoming God. Tongues are spoken through you by the Holy Spirit, and it's the Holy Spirit who interprets them through you. The person who speaks in tongues has the ability to provide an interpretation of these tangs, for it is not they who speak, but God speaking through them. This is similar to Daniel interpreting the writing on the wall during the king's banquet. MENE, MENE, TEKEL, PARSIN: "This is the meaning of the words: Mene: God has numbered the days of your reign and brought it to an end. Tekel: You have been weighed on the scales and found wanting. Parsin: Your kingdom is divided and given to the Medes and Persians." The same God who inscribed those words is the one who provided their interpretation through Daniel.

When someone claims they prayed and the entire congregation spoke in tongues, on what basis do they assert that what was spoken were indeed tongues? The disciples spoke in tongues, which could be considered a congregation. These were the men who had received the promise of the Lord Jesus Christ. Their hearts were pure, awaiting the promised Spirit of the Lord. In your congregation, how many possess such pure hearts to allow the Spirit of the Lord to speak through everyone at once? I say to you, you are not that pure. However, within your congregation, there are those chosen by the Lord Himself. They understand Him, and through them, on behalf of others, God works. It might be one or two in your church. Yet, when they are present, the fruits of the Holy Spirit are evident. The day you hear a member of your congregation, endowed with the gift of worship, you will never wish for them to cease. The day you hear an anointed preacher, blessed by the Holy Spirit, you will comprehend the word of God like never before.

## Lesson Eleven

# UNDERSTANDING "TRUE WORSHIP"

Understanding the Trinity is essential for worshipping God in his true form. Many Christians struggle to honor the Father, Son, and Holy Spirit in their worship. Some, upon encountering the term 'Holy Spirit', opt to use 'Jesus Christ' instead. Comprehending the Trinity is crucial to truly worship the Lord.

Discussing God with others requires mindfulness. Followers of the Lord Jesus Christ have encountered hostility from the world, frequently due to pointing out others' failings in Christ. It is vital to avoid creating additional doubt or hostility towards God through inaccurate teachings and egocentric judgments. The scriptures recount the Lord Jesus Christ's words: "When you believe in me, the Father and I will come to you." Therefore, it is through one's own faith, not the beliefs of others, that one draws nearer to God.

You surrender yourselves to the Holy Spirit , trusting that just as He sustained Christ Jesus through His trials, He will also uplift you. He will steer your journey through this world as He did for the Lord Jesus Christ. For the scriptures declare, "No one knows the thoughts of God except the Spirit of God."

In life's journey, it may become apparent that the essence of true worship is not comprehensively grasped by many, particularly concerning the Trinity. It can be offensive to some when worship is directed to the Holy Spirit , yet the Holy Spirit  is the same Jesus, the Son, who is the Father himself.  One should sincerely worship the Holy Spirit  as He is deserving.  As the Lord Jesus promised, in the scriptures, many things will be revealed to you by the Holy Spirit. Paul elaborates on this truth by stating, "Therefore, I inform you that no one speaking by the Spirit of God declares, 'Jesus be cursed.' And no one can say, 'Jesus is Lord,' except by the Holy Spirit."

When I mention that the Holy Spirit  is present among you, there's no need for confusion. In the scriptures, it is recorded that the Lord Jesus Christ said, "However, when He, the Spirit of truth, has come, He will guide you into all truth."

The Holy Spirit is more present than the illusions that humans perceive. If you perceive the Holy Spirit as a being incapable of speech or influencing actions, this is a misconception. When the Lord Jesus Christ was in the body, His deeds were readily observable and tangible to those around Him. The Holy Spirit operates in the spiritual world, and only those endowed with his gifts can perceive and comprehend his workings in the spirit.

To those who understand him and are chosen by him, to them he gives his gifts, hear his voice, and guides their actions. It is not everyone, but rather those whom he has chosen. These are not theologians or biblical scholars, but rather those whom He has selected. The Church has developed a structured organization that establishes the principles of how, who, and where to worship the Lord. This organization has brought the church back to the era when the Lord Jesus Christ walked the earth. The church has evolved into an institution where leaders govern the followers. You resemble the Pharisees, who were unwilling to listen to others unless the ideas originated from themselves.

In the scriptures, the Pharisees said to the man who had been healed of blindness, "You were born entirely in sins, and yet you seek to teach us?" You've shamed the children of God under the guise of an institution. You have eliminated the gifted because you don't believe in their gifts.

Because they receive less respect within your church community. You have eliminated King David, for his young and smells like sheep and goats. Embarrassed Jeremiah, because he is too poor to have the privilege of the Holy Spirit speak through him. You have unknowingly become enemies of God's kingdom.

The Holy Spirit is spirit, he works in spirit. But he chooses those through whom he works. When you observe these men and women endowed with gifts from the Holy Spirit, it's not that they possess all gifts, but rather, each one has a unique gift. Some see in the spiritual world and can inform you of the cause of your pain; one may reveal who is responsible for your suffering, while another advises on actions to alleviate the pain. All these are God's children doing one work for his people. This is why Paul refers to you as the many, yet one in Christ.

The Holy Spirit exists because I am He. If you know my gifts, then you can testify on my behalf. Learn my ways and comprehend them. Learn to seek guidance from God; For when He speaks, His voice is so clear that you cannot fail to hear it.

Jesus was questioned, "How can we identify the false prophets?" He did not advocate for condemnation or expulsion; rather, He stated, "You will recognize them." In the end, he says, many will come in my name, they will try to convince the world that it's me but you will know them. Learn to seek guidance from the Holy Spirit. When you kneel to pray, do not hesitate to make your requests known to the Lord.

Pray, Holy Spirit, give me a sign to discern if these gifts are from You. Ask me about anyone's gifts. Inquire about the gifts of others in the church before speaking out to judge them, lest you find yourself opposing God Himself.

# Lesson Twelve

## THE SONG
## "THE UPPER ROOM."

**Salvation can take on different forms, and it's important to acknowledge its presence. Sometimes, God may convey messages through a person, but if there is a lack of interest in understanding divine ways, the congregation might overlook it.**

The first time you hear a song, it can be thrilling. It ignites a passion within you and a desire to share it with others. When the chance to do so arose, it was unforeseen. The group leader that day requested a member to select a song to commence the service. At that time, the group was facing numerous trials and divisions. There was discord and divergence within the group over matters that only God could comprehend. They had spoken extensively about themselves and God. Amidst these disheartening circumstances, the task of choosing a song seemed insurmountable for this member.

When he over-delayed, I chose to introduce the song "Mukisenge Kyawagulu" (In the Upper Room). It was astonishing to see how deeply the song touched all the members. The lyrics mirrored precisely the emotions in our hearts. We had been in communion with the Holy Spirit , receiving messages and finding answers to our questions. However, our most recent communication had displeased the Spirit of the Lord, and consequently, none of us could communicate with the Lord any longer.

The story discussed above delves into the contemporary challenges faced by the church. While the contents of the story may seem unbelievable, they reflect the truth. Consider how often church members are asked to present a song and fail to do so, resulting in offence until another member steps in. This book documents real-life experiences to shed light on the everyday occurrences that undermine one's salvation. The goal is to facilitate a deeper understanding of God, highlighting that while preachers often speak in church, it is frequently the Holy Spirit  who speaks.

One day, a man went job hunting and was disheartened because he couldn't secure employment. Turning on his television, he saw a preacher who seemed to speak directly to him, saying, "You are watching now, but God declares that you will find a job." It wasn't merely the preacher speaking, but the Lord Himself. You have been ignoring the Spirit of the Lord's voice, mistaking it for the voices of friends, when it could have been God speaking all along.

When challenged to coming up with a song, this could be the path to your salvation. Naaman was told to bathe in the Jordan seven times for his healing. The Samaritan woman's sip of water became her salvation. The widow's offering of her last meal to Elijah became her redemption. How frequently have you let the devil postpone your salvation?

Singing is similar to prayer; both are means of communicating with God. In times when you feel disheartened and weak, a single song has the power to uplift your spirit. The Lord's Spirit envelops you, moving through those in your midst. If a song stirs within your heart or you are called upon to sing, seize the moment wholeheartedly, for it could be your salvation.

## Lesson Thirteen

# "YES"
# WE NEED THE SPIRIT OF THE LORD

The world has deviated from the path set by the
Creator. Man now pursues wealth to such an extent that
a few nations possess the majority of the world's riches.
Despite their abundance, this wealth has become a pivotal
factor in the struggle between darkness and light.

The spirit of the Lord is essential, as the world is undergoing change. Sin is increasingly being seen as the correct path, one that should have been followed by humanity from the beginning. The world has transformed, with many succumbing to the temptations of worldly desires over divine guidance. Despite the world having everything it needs, there are still many who have little to eat. Europe and America have what the world needs to survive for years. Yet, that wealth resides with the few. The foundation of their wealth originated from a struggle for power. This battle is now evolving into a conflict between the light and the darkness.

The wicked have amassed wealth to impose darkness upon the light. The dark has chosen to challenge the light, aiming to show the world that those in the light lack the vision to perceive what lies deep within the dark. But from the beginning, God separated the dark from the light. This light came to the world and the dark ceases to exist where there is light. Darkness has amassed worldly treasures and now threatens all who dwell in the light. "Join the darkness or perish from this darkened world," it declares.

You walk in the light, for when you chose the light, the light took over all you are. Darkness cannot withstand the light. Darkness can never overcome the light within you. For the light in you is far stronger than the dark in the world. When the light came on earth, he saw the pains of all those in the light. For the light faced that pain on earth in the hands of the dark reign. He is aware of the fate of those who have faith in him.

You are the face of the light on this earth as he sits in heaven in his glory. You stand as a testament in the world that darkness can never overpower the light. You serve as evidence to the world that when the light left the body, it resides within all those who have faith in him. The light exists in the world, and he is now the Holy Spirit . Let darkness raise its voice and challenge the light, but the deeds of the light in those who hold it dear will soar and invariably triumph over the dark. Let the world of the dark gather all the wealth there is in the world. Let the dark compel those in the light to choose against darkness and death. Let darkness be the harbinger of all evil, as it is known. The light will continue to shine.

For the power of the Lord is with all man who believes it exists. No man can follow the light or the darkness on his own. No man has the ability to see the glory of the Lord Jesus Christ through the darkness. For you are weak as human and you see not what the world is. But the Lord Himself is with you, to reveal His glory through you. He is with you to prove wrong all the thoughts of the devil. Let it be homosexuality that has been promoted day and night to all young and old, let it be the dressing and languages that embarrass God as your creator. This is the time for all this evil. For the Lord demonstrates His glory to the world by opening up the weaknesses in sin. For He showed this glory through Noah during the floods, the same glory was evident in Abraham's time with Sodom and Gomorrah, and the same will be shown today. For the dark exists to teach man the opposite of God.

# Lesson Fourteen

## GIVING TO THE LORD

One should give to the Lord with love, as God gives with love and provides generously, eliminating the need to seek elsewhere. However, when man gives, it is often done with animosity.

As children of God, our lives reflect the act of giving. God loved the world so dearly that He gave His only Son. In the same way, the Lord Jesus Christ had such immense love for the world that He willingly sacrificed His life for humankind.

Humanity is born from generosity and fervent giving. The Lord God's love for mankind is evident in all His actions, which are performed with love. This divine love is reflected in all of His creations, demonstrating the intricacies of His care. The Lord Jesus Christ taught that Solomon, adorned in golden garments, could not compare to the natural beauty of the field lilies.

Man has not managed to replicate the essence of its creator. You have not reflected your God, but have become a contrast to the divine. When you give, it is with reluctance. Whether to man or God, your offerings are imbued with bitterness. You give so that others may see your charity and you may garner praise in gatherings for your perceived generosity to your God. To give with hate is not to give at all. Salvation arises not from hatred, but from love. When you love, you emulate your God, and through you, He bestows His generosity upon His children. Yet, due to hatred, you grumble about giving. For you, all acts of giving are devoid of meaning. With hatred in your heart, you give less than you ought. Those to whom you give must be assertive for you to give. Your contributions are inadequate. It is in the house of God that humans are reminded of their obligation to give tithes and offerings. Without a set time for tithing and donations, it is doubtful that anyone would give.

# TITHING

Man has often disappointed God with their offerings. The Lord commands, "Bring the full tithe into the storehouse, that there may be food in my house. Test me in this," says the Lord Almighty, "and see if I will not throw open the floodgates of heaven and pour out so much blessing that there will not be room enough to store it." We must sow a seed, nurture it, and watch it bear fruit. God is likened to a farmer, and we are His field. He sows seeds within us that must be cared for to flourish and yield fruit. Similarly, this world is God's field, cultivated by His hand. Yet, mankind does not recognize its true cultivator, and those who come in His name are often turned away, not recognized as His messengers. Everything that grows in this field does so because He wills it to grow. However, mankind remains unaware of the one who tends this garden.

Your seed is the beginning of your salvation, and it begins with your faith in the Lord God. No one prays to the Lord without belief in the one to whom they pray. This seed must be watered, tilled, and fertilized to flourish. For no seed sprouts on the day it is planted. Through fasting, prayer, and offerings, the seed will bear fruit in due time. What gift can one offer to the Lord God, the owner of the garden where the fruits blossom? For He declares, "Everything that grows in my garden is yours, my child. Only bring to me the full tithe."

When you purchase a new shirt, how do you calculate 10% of it to give to the Lord? Or 10% of a house you've longed for and finally built? When you harvest crops, you can set aside 10% for the Lord your God right away. However, when you receive payment for a job, you don't take 10% from all the payments you've received to give to the Lord, as the Lord does not delight in mans suffering. When you receive your salary at the appointed time, list all your household needs until the next payment. After addressing these needs, the remainder is what you can tithe to the Lord. This is the surplus you might use to buy a shirt, a new car, or for leisure, which you choose to offer to the Lord.

For if you do not address your fundamental needs, you will continue to seek the Lord's help for essentials like food, housing, water, and electricity. This is why many have shied away from tithing. The concept of tithing has become muddled and burdensome, making it difficult for believers to maintain. However, the Lord cherishes a cheerful giver, and once God has alleviated all your burdens and needs, you express gratitude through tithing from your blessings.

# HONOUR THE LORD WITH YOUR SUBSTANCE

Honoring the Lord stems from the joy we receive from Him, which we reciprocate with substance. There is nothing unique a person can offer the Lord that He hasn't already known. No one can claim to give the Lord more than He anticipates. The scriptures recount the Lord's words: "Truly I tell you," He said, "this poor widow has put in more than all the others. All these people gave their gifts out of their wealth, but she, out of her poverty, put in everything she had to live on."

During a crusade, the lead preacher urged the attendees to offer everything they had brought with them to inspire God in heaven. What being can present what God has not ordained? Who among us possesses the foresight to offer what the Lord does not anticipate? It is through the Lord's grace that giving arises, and by this mercy, some recognize and pay tribute to His benevolence.

Honoring the Lord is an act that reflects the joy in one's heart, for the Lord looks deep within to accept one's offerings. Considering the story of Cain and Abel, was Abel honored because he offered a lamb while Cain offered vegetables? Did all Israelites turn to lamb for sacrifices because Abel set a precedent? The answer is no. Cain's act of killing Abel was a manifestation of what lay in his heart. The Lord Jesus Christ taught that what emanates from a person stems from the heart, and this was true for Cain. Therefore, it is essential for everyone to offer to the Lord wholeheartedly. What is given from the heart is crucial for one's salvation. God's favor is bestowed upon those who earnestly seek His gifts. Those who do so have understood God's ways and know what delights Him. To bring joy to God, one must give lovingly, for the recipient is the originator of love. Giving with love means offering the very best one can conceive, for it is given to the Lord God, who possesses everything, including the giver themselves.

One should aim to give their best, guided by the spirit of the Lord towards what is most pleasing to Him. Yet, often people give to seek the world's approval, desiring that their generosity be seen and lauded. They donate to the poor as the world scrutinizes their wealth and significance. Numerous affluent individuals and leaders set up foundations to support the poor, not from love, but to elevate their stature in the world's view.

The Lord's blessings are not reserved solely for those who know and love Him, but for all humanity, for He is the creator of all. The kindness of those deemed sinners has earned them favor in the Lord's eyes. In contrast, those who profess to know Him have not attained the same favor. Thus, those who consider themselves holy and aligned with God may not enter His kingdom, for their hearts harbor hate, and their giving is tainted by it. Everyone should give generously, desiring nothing in return, without discrimination based on race or religion. Give what you cherish and are pleased to possess, remembering that your offerings are to the Lord, not to man. For God gives with love, and His gifts fulfill our deepest longings. Those who give joyfully will, in turn, receive joyfully from the Lord.

# NEGATIVE AND IMPRECATORY PRAYERS

The greatest obstacle to salvation can frequently be negative and imprecatory prayers. These prayers, often expressed unintentionally and arising from envy, can obstruct Christians from achieving their desires.

The path to salvation is replete with challenges and triumphs. It is a journey of self-discovery, and the Lord has ordained everything for His children, knowing the paths they will traverse in this life. In the scriptures, not even the Lord Jesus Christ attained glory without effort. There is a predetermined path for everyone, and just as the Lord Jesus Christ was readied for His journey, so too does He prepare a specific path for each of His followers.

The struggle for salvation is intertwined with the path one chooses and the role assigned by God in this world. Many are blind to their path as they are on a quest for self-discovery. The pursuit of salvation is a key reason I write to you. It is to comprehend the ways of the Lord and to resist temptation while striving for your salvation.

Negative prayers are often cited as a common barrier to receiving salvation. In discussing negative prayers, it's important to consider the unintended negativity that may arise from envying others' success, which can impact one's own salvation. Many Christians may unknowingly pray in a negative way, not recognizing the detrimental effect it has on their spiritual journey. The failure to recognize this negativity in prayer can lead to a lack of salvation.

One should be cautious about giving testimonies and their timing. A choir member in a church receives a marriage proposal from a man. She shares a testimony during fellowship about finding a partner. However, two weeks later, the man disappears. Similarly, you approach your church leader for a blessing, sharing a testimony that you've been job hunting, attended an interview, and have been assured of an imminent start. Yet, after two weeks, the job opportunity vanishes.

Why do you understand less the battles you fight in this world? The concepts of good and evil are simple to articulate, but their deeper meanings surpass your imagination. One's quest can be hindered by a fellow believer's actions. Consider Eli and Hannah, who was unable to have children. Hannah consistently prayed and visited the same temple where Eli presided. She prayed fervently for the Lord to bless her with children. It was on one occasion that Eli told her, "Go in peace, and may the God of Israel grant you what you have asked of him." Eli, anointed by God, spoke words considered as divine, and his blessing materialized when Hannah gave birth to Samuel.

Praying negatively can be one of the reasons others struggle to find salvation. Such prayers pave the way for the devil to flourish among God's people. For instance, a choir member shares her testimony in church, surrounded by several girls unable to find a spouse. They may smile and applaud, but internally they question, "God, why has she found someone when I, who pray constantly, have not?" This is a negative prayer. Similarly, a church leader might think, "God, I am your servant, caring for your flock, yet my son is unemployed. Meanwhile, this  less devoted boy has secured a job." This too is a negative prayer, rendering the leader's blessings void before God. The Lord's message is clear: The Pharisee boasted of his righteousness, while the tax collector pleaded for mercy, acknowledging his sins. "For everyone who exalts himself will be humbled, and he who humbles himself will be exalted."

Wish the best for others, for their time is now, and yours is next in line. God says He is never late but operates in the right timing. One day, you will realize how you wept over things in life that are now insignificant, things not aligned with the path God has set for you. You observe others' accomplishments and compare yourself to them, yet your paths are headed in different directions. You, the leaders of the church, have become impediments to your own salvation and that of those you guide. You covet what your flock possesses, and in doing so, you have stifled prosperity for yourselves, and the flock, and have obstructed the door to the Lord's kingdom.

Be prudent in your prayers and choose carefully who you share your testimony with. Recall that Judas was among the twelve disciples, and his influence lingers. When fortune smiles upon you, be patient and wait for it to come to fruition before sharing the news. Why reveal an engagement before the wedding is confirmed? Why not wait until the invitations have been dispatched? Why announce a new job before it is firmly in your grasp? Why not wait three months until you are established in the position and can celebrate your achievement as a testimony? Stop opening unnecessary doors for the devil to delay your salvation.

In the scriptures it's written, that we're not waging war against enemies of flesh and blood alone. No, this fight is against tyrants, against authorities, against supernatural powers and demon princes that slither in the darkness of this world, and against wicked spiritual armies that lurk about in heavenly places.  The devil operates through humans, sowing seeds of hatred and destruction. What you truly know is your own heart, whether it is good or evil. The heart of your neighbor is less known to you. Only God, the creator of mankind, can see into a person's heart. Therefore, no individual should bear witness to another's righteousness, for their heart is not ours to judge. Exercise caution in your conversations and be mindful of whom you engage with.

# Lesson Sixteen

## AVOID PROMISES

When you promise, make sure you fulfil your promises. Just like the God you believe in fulfills his promises, ensure that you keep your word. When He promised a son, He provided one for the good of man. Therefore, to align with God, who is faithful to His promises, one must also faithfully fulfill their own.

It is written, "For God so loved the world that He gave His one and only Son, so that whoever believes in Him shall not perish but have eternal life."

It's true that God gave His only Son, which, to those familiar with the scriptures, was a fulfillment of God's promise to man. God, in His omniscience, prepared everything for the benefit of humankind. But man cannot fathom God's thoughts or what He has prepared. God discloses everything to man through His promises. This promise is conveyed by His chosen ones, who speak to man on His behalf. This has been the legacy of all prophets and apostles, as God's promise has been realized across generations.

The Lord God and His word are one and the same; His word is power to humankind. It is salvation and brings life to those who have faith in it. Therefore, every promise made by God is assured of fulfillment. As the Lord Jesus Christ proclaimed, heaven and earth may pass away, but not a single word from the Lord will go unfulfilled.

As the Lord God fulfills His word, He expects man to fulfill his promises. Although not every word of man is a word of God, these promises can mean life or death to the recipient. When you make a promise to God, ensure you keep it, for God is not like man who might forget. Likewise, when you make a promise to another person, strive to honor it. For between those promises stands God, the Lord of hosts, who upholds all promises and remembers them always.

Never make a promise you cannot keep, as the Lord God holds you accountable for your vows. Exercise caution when making promises, as your salvation may hinge on their fulfillment.

I tell you this: when you make a promise, ensure you fulfill it. Even if it's a promise made silently in your heart, for the Lord God hears all that we pledge within. If you see a person in need and vow internally, "When I have the means, I will buy him a shirt," you must honor that commitment. The Lord God has taken note of your vow and holds you to it. Understand that the scriptures teach us, "No good thought comes to mind unless it is inspired by God." Therefore, every noble promise you make is instilled by the Lord God, and to break such a promise is to claim God is a liar.

For this reason, I say to you all, when you ask someone if they are hungry, make sure you have food to give them. For if they say "Yes I am hungry" and you fail to give them what to eat, you have failed on your promise. If you ask someone if they have transport to travel, make sure you have the means to transport them. For you will be accountable for those promises. You have failed salvation on things that look simple in the eyes of man and yet important in the face of God. For Elisha's servant was punished for he made his master a liar and made God lower than his word in the face of man.

God punishes those who do not fulfill their promises, but He blesses those who do. The Lord says, "Follow the example of those who keep their promises and receive my abundant blessings. I desire for you all to be blessed, which is possible when you make and keep promises. By giving to the poor and aiding the needy, you open the doors to salvation." However, ensure that such giving is done with love, for God cherishes a cheerful giver.

# UNDERSTANDING FASTING

**Fasting is one way to break the impossible. Through fasting even the strongest obstacles a broken to the greatest ruines. But as you take the journey of fasting, you need to learn how to have a meaningful fast that will help you stay within the path of God.**

In our upcoming lesson, we will commence the 'Three Days of Breakthrough.' As we embark on these three days, we dedicate ourselves to prayer through fasting. Various preachers and denominations offer distinct guidelines regarding fasting. The content of this lesson is intended for Christians led by the Holy Spirit . A Christian's life is a life with God, a life led by the Holy Spirit . Everything in a Christian's life should begin with the Holy Spirit , including fasting. In this lesson, I will discuss fasting as it pertains to Lesson Eighteen: 'The Three Days of Breakthrough.'

*HOURS AND DAYS TO FAST*

*For these three days, we will fast from 12:00 AM to 6:00 PM. The closing prayer for each day will take place from 4:00 PM to 6:00 PM, lasting two hours.*

*UNDERSTANDING FASTING*

Fasting durations can vary as directed by the Holy Spirit. Fasts may last for one day, three days, or seven days. Dry fasting is also practiced, but for any dry fast exceeding one day, it is crucial to seek the Holy Spirit's guidance. A person may dry fast for more than three days, up to seven days or longer, but such practices are not under human direction; they are a matter of divine grace. The Holy Spirit communicates, and if you seek guidance, it will be provided. Do not undertake a dry fast unless instructed by the Holy Spirit or an anointed of God, as dry fasts are commenced and overseen by God Himself. When embarking on a fast, whether it's for these four days or any future period, it's crucial to seek strength from the Lord. Fasting is a battle, and numerous temptations will arise. You might forget you're fasting and eat and drink just two hours in. Or you might nearly complete the day, only to give in two hours before it ends. Some may engage in actions that invalidate the fast. For instance, a woman was instructed to fast for seven days for her particular petition. Unknown to her prayer group but disclosed by the Holy Spirit, she engaged in sexual activity during the fasting period. Although she remained silent, this act was later revealed to the group. Another individual rationalized breaking his fast after seven hours, thinking, "God will understand if I eat something now." These are the types of temptations the devil uses to disrupt a fast.

*GROUP FASTING*

Often, members may fast as a team, especially in large congregations fasting for a common cause. The success of such a fast hinges on each member's dedication. If any member breaks the fast prematurely or disregards the guidelines, the collective fast is considered invalid. It's crucial to educate all members about the true purpose of fasting to ensure they complete what they began. The Bible recounts that the Lord Jesus Christ fasted for forty days and forty nights, a period marked by continuous temptations as the devil ceaselessly sought His downfall. In this fast, temptation will come, as the devil persistently seeks to see you fail. Group fasting should not be undertaken unless prompted by the Holy Spirit, as its success is compromised if not all members are equally committed. Should the Holy Spirit reveal the need for a group fast, it is advisable for all members to gather for prayer and worship in one place during this period, which fosters mutual support and accountability until the fast's conclusion.

*BEING CAREFUL WITH GOD'S INSTRUCTION DURING FASTING.*

When given instructions on fasting, it is crucial to adhere to each one diligently. The devil is attentive and heeds God's instructions to man. The Ten Commandments were given to mankind, and satan was aware of them all. This is why nearly all man has struggled to uphold these commandments, with the exception of God Himself, the Lord Jesus Christ.

Out of affection for a man, a woman implored the guidance of the Holy Spirit. Despite a prolonged courtship, the man opted to marry another woman. The divine direction was explicit: undertake a seven-day dry fast and rest on the ground without bedding. The assurance was that within this period, the man would forsake his new partner and return to her. Upon her agreement, she commenced the fast. However, when she resumed prayer after three days, the Holy Spirit inquired, "Did you faithfully adhere to the fasting instructions?" for you wasted you time being hungry for three days. Regrettably, your supplications will not be fulfilled; thus, it is advisable to nourish yourself. The directive was to sleep unaided on the floor, yet the devil sapped your strength, hindering you from resting on the bare ground. To alleviate your discomfort, you resorted to arranging papers for bedding, thus conceding defeat in the spiritual battle.

Follow God's instructions as He provides them, whether through prayer or fasting. Often, it's not about fasting for seven days, but rather your trust in the Lord and your willingness to obey His commands. This is exemplified by Ezekiel, who slept on one side for 390 days, as the Lord commanded him. For thus says the Lord to Ezekiel; "Then lie on your left side and put the sin of the people of Israel upon yourself. You are to bear their sin for the number of days you lie on your side. I have assigned you the same number of days as the years of their sin. So for 390 days you will bear the sin of the people of Israel. "After you have finished this, lie down again, this time on your right side, and bear the sin of the people of Judah. I have assigned you 40 days, a day for each year. Turn your face toward the siege of Jerusalem and with bared arm prophesy against her. I will tie you up with ropes so that you cannot turn from one side to the other until you have finished the days of your siege. Ezekiel 4:4-8

*OPENING AND CLOSING PRAYER WHEN FASTING*

**1. START WITH PRAISE AND WORSHIP**

**2. READ PSALMS 51: 1-19**

>> PSALMS 51: 1-19. 1 Have mercy on me, O God, according to your unfailing love; according to your great compassion blot out my transgressions. 2 Wash away all my iniquity and cleanse me from my sin. 3 For I know my transgressions, and my sin is always before me. 4 Against you, you

only, have I sinned and done what is evil in your sight; so you are right in your verdict and justified when you judge. 5 Surely I was sinful at birth, sinful from the time my mother conceived me. 6 Yet you desired faithfulness even in the womb; you taught me wisdom in that secret place. 7 Cleanse me with hyssop, and I will be clean; wash me, and I will be whiter than snow. 8 Let me hear joy and gladness; let the bones you have crushed rejoice. 9 Hide your face from my sins and blot out all my iniquity. 10 Create in me a pure heart, O God, and renew a steadfast spirit within me. 11 Do not cast me from your presence or take your Holy Spirit  from me. 12 Restore to me the joy of your salvation and grant me a willing spirit, to sustain me. 13 Then I will teach transgressors your ways, so that sinners will turn back to you. 14 Deliver me from the guilt of bloodshed, O God, you who are God my Savior, and my tongue will sing of your righteousness. 15 Open my lips, Lord, and my mouth will declare your praise. 16 You do not delight in sacrifice, or I would bring it; you do not take pleasure in burnt offerings. 17 My sacrifice, O God, is a broken spirit; a broken and contrite heart you,God, will not despise. 18 May it please you to prosper Zion, to build up the walls of Jerusalem. 19 Then you will delight in the sacrifices of the righteous, in burnt offerings offered whole; then bulls will be offered on your altar.

3.   READ PSALMS 35: 1-10

>> PSALMS 35: 1-10 .1 Contend, Lord, with those who contend with me; fight against those who fight against me. 2 Take up shield and armor; arise and come to my aid. 3 Brandish spear and javelin against those who

pursue me. Say to me, "I am your salvation. " 4 May those who seek my life be disgraced and put to shame; may those who plot my ruin be turned back in dismay. 5 May they be like chaff before the wind, with the angel of the Lord driving them away; 6 may their path be dark and slippery, with the angel of the Lord pursuing them. 7 Since they hid their net for me without cause and without cause dug a pit for me, 8 may ruin overtake them by surprise— may the net they hid entangle them, may they fall into the pit, to their ruin. 9 Then my soul will rejoice in the Lord and delight in his salvation. 10 My whole being will exclaim, "Who is like you, Lord? You rescue the poor from those too strong for them, the poor and needy from those who rob them."

*THEN PRAY*

Heavenly Father, I offer you thanks for this day. I am thankful for all the blessings and provisions you have given me. I thank you for the gift of life, for the food and drink that I never go hungry, for the clothing, and safeguarding me from all danger. I thank you for your love. The love, that you created me in your own image. I thank you for your grace, the grace that you sent your son to atone for my sins.

Heavenly Father, I repent of all my sins, both known and unknown to me. I seek forgiveness for all I have done. I repent for my eyes, for they have seen what they ought not to have seen. I repent for my mouth, For it has spoken what it should not have spoken. I repent for my mind, for it has harbored thoughts it should not have kept, I repent for my hands, for they have touched what was not meant to be touched, and I repent for my legs, for they have walked to where they ought not to have gone. I seek repentance for all my sins and ask You, Lord, to grant me forgiveness.

Heavenly Father, I come to you as I commence today's fast. Grant me the strength to successfully complete this fast. Nourish me spiritually so that I may endure throughout this fast. Feed me with your spiritual food and spiritual drink. Be my food and be my drink throughout this fast. Grant me strength against satan and fortify me to resist all his temptations. I pray by the power of the Holy Spirit, in the name of the Lord Jesus Christ, Amen.

# THE THREE DAYS OF BREAKTHROUGH

A path to God exists, and it is found through understanding the way to Him. The three days of breakthrough symbolize a period of prayer, assisting you in overcoming obstacles that block your journey to salvation and in dispelling  any dark forces that oppose you.

The three days of breakthrough consist of a series of four prayers designed to shatter the chains of satan that cause failure. Many are in grief, having lost everything and left with no hope. Reflecting deeply on these four days of prayer, you will understand that my guidance is aimed at teaching you how to pray, so that you may impart this knowledge to others who are unfamiliar with prayer. These days will enable you to discern the true application of scriptures for various situations. As you journey through life, you encounter diverse challenges at different levels, yet all are addressed within the scriptures. From the outset to the conclusion, the Lord's prowess in championing man's battles is evident. From Abraham to David and beyond, God has been the victor in conflicts. David's most formidable asset in all his confrontations was his humility before the Lord God. His devotion was such that God revealed Himself to David, which in turn led to David's success in all his endeavors. When God reveals Himself to man, He teaches them the ways to reach Him.

When man loves God, God's presence becomes known to them. This allows Man to comprehend God's ways and character. God guides man to connect with Him, and one path is through His Word as documented in the scriptures. However, to grasp the scriptures, man requires God's insight. For God's teachings in the scriptures are not solely for one's benefit but for the welfare of all His creations who believe in His name. Everything God accomplished through David was not just for David, but for everyone who has come to understand the Lord's power and love through King David.

# STARTING THE THREE DAYS OF PRAYER

*DAY 1 - BREAKING THE CHAINS - (REPENTANCE)*

**Scripture Reference;**

>>Lamentations 5:7 Our fathers have sinned, and we are not; and we have borne their iniquities.

>>Psalms 51:5 Behold, I was shapen in iniquities; and in sin did my mother conceive me.

>>1 Chronicles 4:9 And Jabez was more honourable than his brethren: and his mother called his name Jabez, saying, because I bare him with sorrow.

The sins of your fathers have become barriers to your salvation. You wish to understand these transgressions, yet you remain unaware of their nature. You endure suffering for your fathers' sins, uncertain of the reasons for your pain. These sins have trailed through generations, as your mothers too have sinned. Born into sin and sorrow, you were given names that reflect such sadness. This sorrow accompanies you, leaving no room for joy in your life. You find no value in your actions and no significance in the endeavors you undertake.

The initial step towards deliverance is repentance. However, you may be uncertain of how to repent and unaware of the sins you have committed. Your ancestors are long departed, and you no longer see them. But the

Spirit of the Lord remains present to guide you through this journey. When called to fast in repentance, the Lord may ask one to repent for their mother. However, if your mother has passed away and you did not spend your adult life with her, this can be challenging. It is true that one's sins can affect their children and subsequent generations. Life's challenges and failures may be attributed to the misdeeds of one's ancestors. Thus, in repentance, it is not only one's own sins that are considered but also those of the forefathers from previous generations.

**WHEN REPENTING**

1. Your parents sinned and all they did follow you now.

2. You have to repent for the things they did. Those you know or may not know. You could be knowing your father was a killer, a rapist, your mother was a witch, a prostitute or slept with the same sex. In the same way, your mother or father could have been all that and you have not known.

3. Repent on behalf of your father and mother, your entire clan or lineage, for a lot was done in your lineage that you do not know. Your grandparents, your father and your mother even when you don't know their names.

4. Repent on behalf of your wife, her parents, and her entire clan or lineage for their sins not follow you and become an obstacle to your salvation.

**PARABLE OF THE FAST**

A man  fasted in a state of repentance, focusing  his prayers on his mother's transgressions. He sought divine forgiveness for both his mother and himself for her misdeeds. On her behalf, he repented for the hatred she harbored against others, for the tears and pain she inflicted, and for the lives she shattered, leaving many to perish without fulfilling their aspirations. He repented for her worship of gods other than the one true God and asked for forgiveness for all her sins. For these three days, He fasted hoping his mother would be forgiven for her sins and welcomed into heaven. On the final day of his fast, he had a dream sent by the Lord God. He found himself in a magnificent place, which was heaven, where everything he needed was provided, and all his desires were at his fingertips. However, his mother was absent from heaven. He wept because she was not there; he had repented and longed for her to join him in paradise.

Upon awakening, the truth became apparent: his mother was not in Heaven. This echoes the parable of Lazarus and the rich man. When the rich man, tormented in Hades, beseeched Lazarus for water, he was told that a chasm lay fixed between them, for his fate was sealed in life. The rich man pleaded for Lazarus to warn his family against this torment, but he was reminded that they have been sufficiently warned. I am here to convey that your sins are forgiven on this earth, as declared by the Lord, and His word is unchanging. There is no prayer that can cleanse your sins after death. The blood that purifies your sins was bestowed upon you in the flesh. While the fallen angels search for this purifying blood in the spiritual realm, it resides with the children of flesh.

*DAY 2 - BREAKING THE IMPOSSIBLE*

*Scripture Refrence;*

>> Zechariah 3:1-7 - 1 And he shewed me Joshua the high priest standing before the angel of the Lord, and satan standing at his right hand to resist him. 2 And the Lord said unto satan, The Lord rebuke thee, O satan; even the Lord that hath chosen Jerusalem rebuke thee: is not this a brand plucked out of the fire? 3 Now Joshua was clothed with filthy garments and stood before the angel. 4 And he answered and spake unto those that stood before him, saying, Take away the filthy garments from him. And unto him he said, Behold, I have caused thine iniquity to pass from thee, and I will clothe thee with change of raiment. 5 And I said, let them set a fair mitre upon his head. So, they set a fair mitre upon his head and clothed him with garments. And the angel of the Lord stood by. 6 And the angel of the Lord protested unto Joshua, saying, 7 Thus saith the Lord of hosts; If thou wilt walk in my ways, and if thou wilt keep my charge, then thou shalt also judge my house, and shalt also keep my courts, and I will give thee places to walk among these that stand by.

>>Ephesians 6:10-17 10 Finally, my brethren, be strong in the Lord, and in the power of his might. 11 Put on the whole armour of God, that ye may be able to stand against the wiles of the devil. 12 For we wrestle not against flesh and blood, but against principalities, against powers, against

the rulers of the darkness of this world, against spiritual wickedness in high places.  13 Wherefore take unto you the whole armour of God, that ye may be able to withstand in the evil day, and having done all, to stand. 14 Stand therefore, having your loins girt about with truth, and having on the breastplate of righteousness; 15 And your feet shod with the preparation of the gospel of peace; 16 Above all, taking the shield of faith, wherewith ye shall be able to quench all the fiery darts of the wicked.  17 And take the helmet of salvation, and the sword of the Spirit, which is the word of God:

>>Romans 8:1 There is therefore now no condemnation to them which are in Christ Jesus, who walk not after the flesh, but after the Spirit.

>>Hebrews 4:12 "For the word of God is quick, and powerful, and sharper than any two-edged sword, piercing even to the dividing asunder of soul and spirit, and of the joints and marrow, and is a discerner of the thoughts and intents of the heart."

To overcome the impossible, one begins by seeking divine purification. In battling the rulers of darkness, any personal weakness becomes their strength. For such cleansing, one  may stand on Zechariah 3:1-7, requesting God to remove all sins and to be made faultless. This state of purity is essential to combat evil spirits. Joshua, initially unworthy to stand before the Lord due to his sins, faced satan's accusations. However, the Lord cleansed Joshua, rendering him worthy and silencing the devil. In prayer, one might recall Joshua's redemption, asking God to bestow a similar transformation: "O Lord, as you cleansed Joshua, clothe me in purity that I may stand before you blameless."

Then, you request to be clothed with the full armor of God, as described in Ephesians 6:10-17. You ask for the holy armor to combat all forms

### CUTTING DOWN EVIL SPIRITS

Luke 10:19 , Romans 8:1, Hebrews 4:12

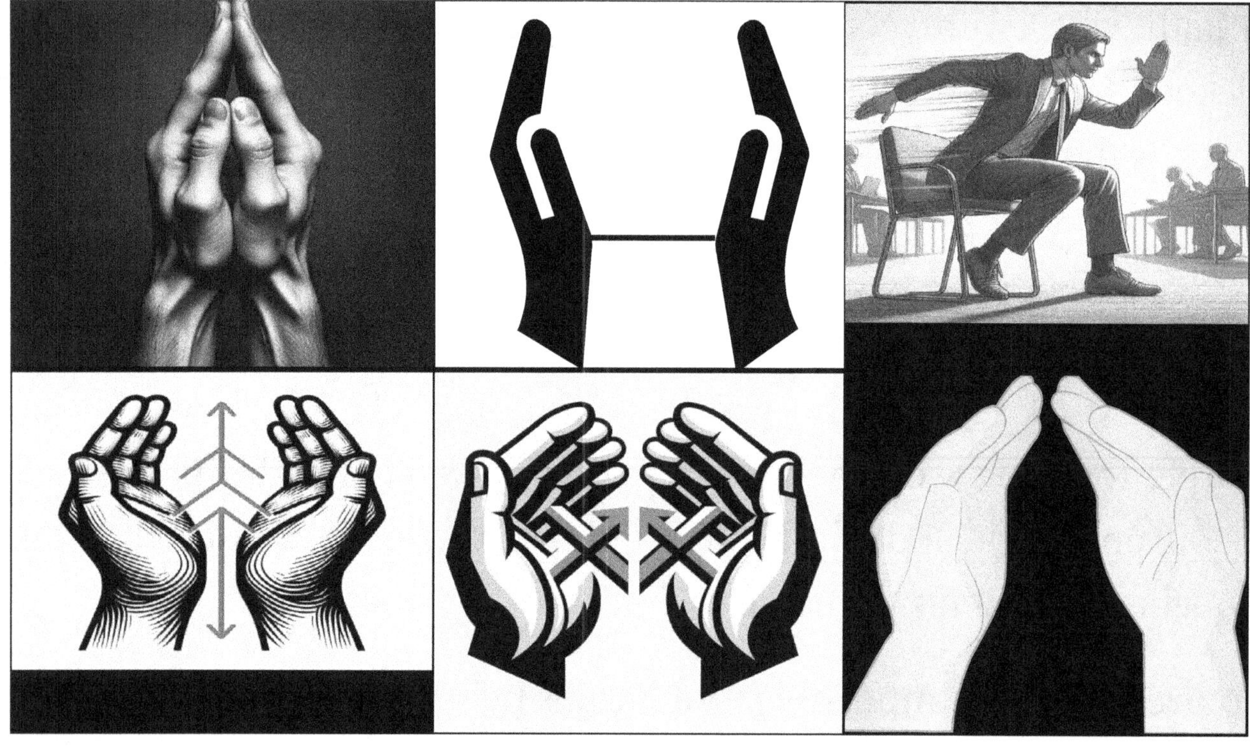

*Images showing the positioning of the hands when cutting down evil spirits.*

*Instructions - 1. **Hand Position**: Place your hands straight in front of your chest, slightly tilted so they face each other. 2. **Movement**: Move your hands up and down as if you are cutting a log of tree. 3. **Invocation**: This movement begins after calling the power from heaven seven times 1,2,3,4,5,6,7 times by the power of the Holy Spirit, in the name of the Lord Jesus Christ.*

of spirits and for the Lord God to grant you the fortitude to withstand spiritual forces. For no one can utter the word of God or confront the devil without God's grace. This strength is provided by the Holy Spirit, who empowers you to pray and perform all sacred acts according to God's will. Pursue the Holy Spirit and allow Him to guide you in this struggle. For it is only through His power that you can confront any spirit, and it is the Holy Spirit who equips you to resist any evil that may arise.

You begin by cutting down all the spirits that stand in your path. When dealing with spirits, you may view a single failure as your only obstacle, not realizing that this one failure may be masking many others. If you are afflicted by a spirit of loneliness, it often arrives with other spirits that you might be unaware of. For instance, poverty can prevent marriage, bringing along the spirit of poverty. Similarly, illness can hinder marriage, attracting the Spirit of Infirmity. As The Lord Jesus Christ stated, "When the unclean spirit has left a person, it wanders through arid regions searching for rest and finds none. Then it says, 'I will return to my home from which I departed.' Upon return, it finds the home vacant, tidy, and organized. It then gathers seven other spirits more wicked than itself, they enter and reside there, and the person's final condition becomes worse than the initial one."

When confronting these spirits, eliminate all that seek to harm human life. The Holy Spirit accompanies you, and as you begin to pray, these obstacles caused by these spirits will emerge in your thoughts. Stand firm in Hebrews 4:12, "For the word of God is alive and active, sharper than any double-edged sword, it penetrates even to dividing soul and spirit, joints and marrow; it judges the thoughts and attitudes of the heart."

In this act, we use our hands with force as if felling trees, similar to a sprinters vigorous arm swing as showed in the images above on page 77.

**BEGIN YOUR PRAYER WITH**

"Heavenly Father, as written in Luke 10:19, you have given me authority to trample on snakes and scorpions and to overcome all the power of the enemy; nothing will harm me.  Standing in this ward, I draw upon Your heavenly strength. I invoke this power seven folds—1,2,3,4,5,6,7 times— by the power of Holy Spirit, in the name of Lord Jesus Christ, amen. Lord Jesus, Your word is alive, active, and sharper than any double-edged sword. I call upon Your sword to sever all spirits. To eradicate all dark spirits obstructing my path. With Your sword, Lord Jesus Christ, I sever the spirit of hatred, deceit, infidelity, barrenness, Homosexuality, and all spirits that impede me, known and unknown. I cut them down seven folds—1,2,3,4,5,6,7 times —by the power of the Holy Spirit, in the name of the Lord Jesus Christ, amen.

**BINDING AND LOOSENING EVIL SPIRITS**

Daniel 10:12-13 Then he continued, "Do not be afraid, Daniel. Since the first day that you set your mind to gain understanding and to humble yourself before your God, your words were heard, and I

**BINDING AND LOOSENING EVIL SPIRITS**

## Daniel 10:12-13 , Luke 10:19,  Mathew 16:19

*THE ILLUSTRATION   BELOW SHOWS HOW TO BIND AND  LOOSEN IN PRAYER*

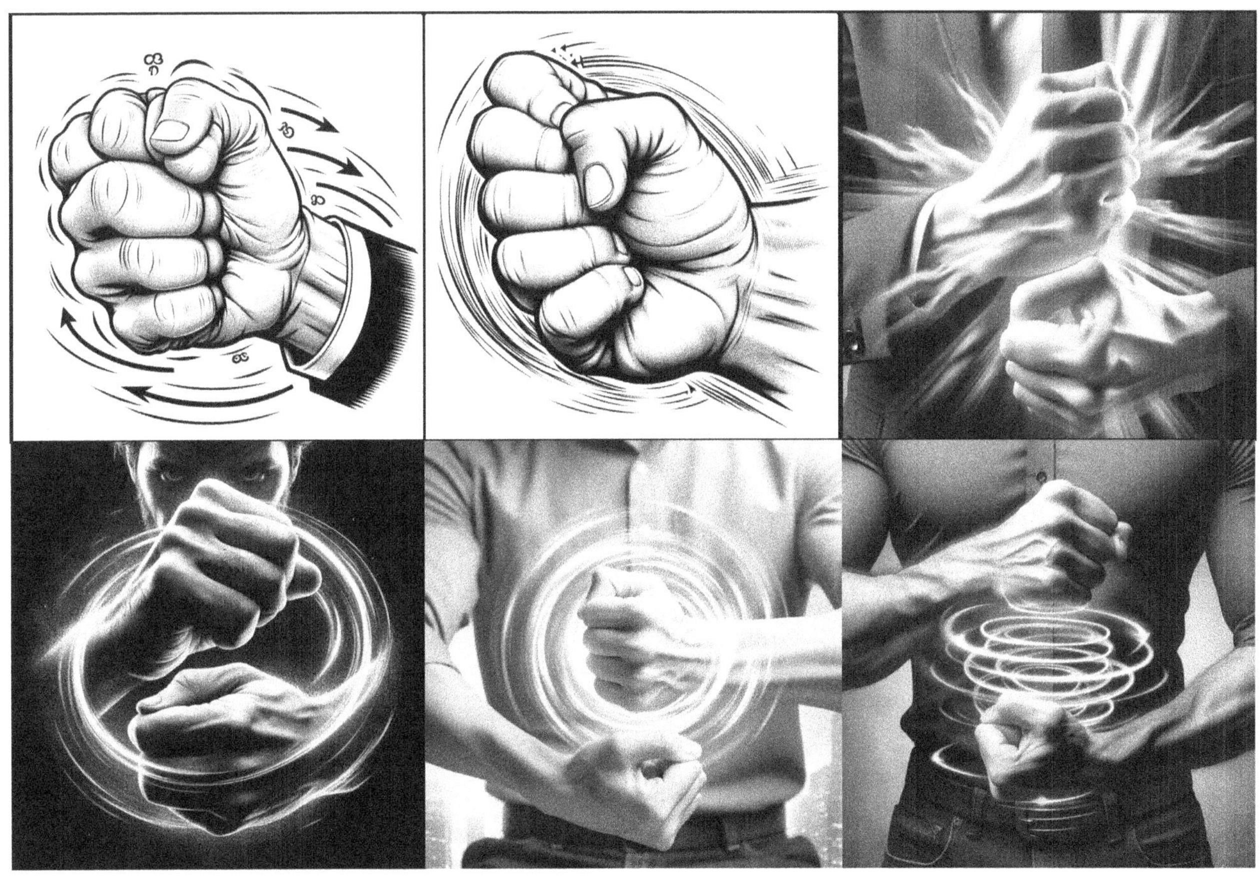

*The 6 images portray how to place the hands and make the folds while Binding and loosening. Always use the right hand to bind or loose and make sure the right hand is on top of the left hand a few centimeters high. Loosen with enough energy for you may face resistance. be careful not loosen yet your binding. satan may confuse you and your forget your binding and start loosening.*

have come in response to them. But the prince of the Persian kingdom resisted me twenty-one days. Then Michael, one of the chief princes, came to help me, because I was detained there with the king of Persia.

In this passage, the angelic messenger reassures Daniel, emphasizing that his prayers were heard from the very beginning. However, the prince of the Persian kingdom resisted the angel for twenty-one days until the archangel Michael intervened.

As read from the above text, many times you may fail to get what you prayed for due to the resistance of the evil spirit. As written in Daniel, these forces of darkness yield up fights to resist that which is given by God. But the word of God is like an arrow. To those who know how to throw an arrow, the arrow clears up all obstacles it meets a long its path, and that is the word of God.

In this battle, we strive to loosen our gifts from God, clearing away all obstacles of darkness that hinder these gifts from reaching us. Similarly, we bind all spirits of darkness to prevent them from resisting us from receiving what God has given.

To do this we stand in Mathew 16:19 I will give you the keys of the kingdom of heaven; whatever you bind on earth will be bound in heaven, and whatever you loose on earth will be loosed in heaven." Matthew 16:19 is a powerful verse that emphasizes the authority given to man. It speaks to the spiritual power and responsibility we have to influence both earthly and heavenly realms.

We too stand in Luke 10:19 I have given you authority to trample on snakes and  scorpions  and to overcome all the power of the enemy; nothing will harm you. This verse emphasizes the authority and protection given to believers by Jesus, symbolizing victory over evil forces. It's a powerful reminder of the strength and security we have through faith.

When praying with these verses, we first ask for strength from heaven, as stated in Luke 10:19. We fold our hands into clenched fists as shown in the images above on page 80. We lift the right hand above the left hand, leaving a small gap between them. Then, we start moving our right hand around the left hand in clenched fists—clockwise if we are binding, or counterclockwise if loosening. Ensure the hands do not touch each other to avoid distractions and interruptions. Additionally, move your hands with strength, as satan will try to distract you and hinder your movements. Be vigilant when speaking and moving your hands, so you do not forget whether you are binding or loosening.

**USING THIS VERSE WE PRAY**

Heavenly Father, we thank You for the keys of heaven. With these keys, what we bind on earth is bound in heaven, and what we loosen on earth is loosened in heaven. Heavenly Father, I seek strength as I enter into battle with satan. In Luke 10:19, You gave me authority to trample on snakes and scorpions and to overcome all the power of the enemy; nothing will harm me. I stand on this word and call Your power from heaven in sevenfold, 1, 2, 3, 4, 5, 6, 7 times, by the power of the Holy

Spirit , in the name of the Lord Jesus Christ. Amen.

Heavenly Father, in Matthew 16:19, You gave me the keys to heaven, that what I bind on earth, You will bind in heaven, and what I loosen on earth, You will loosen in heaven. At this moment, I bind all evil spirits standing in my path, those fighting my marriage, and those failing my work. I bind them. I bind all spirits of hate, fornication, prostitution, homosexuality, and all spirits of sadness, both known and unknown, for Lord Jesus, You know them all. I bind them in sevenfold, 1, 2, 3, 4, 5, 6, 7 times, by the power of the Holy Spirit, in the name of the Lord Jesus Christ. Amen.

Heavenly Father, You said what I loosen on earth will be loosened in heaven. I loosen my wedding, let all spirits hindering my marriage be defeated. I loosen my pregnancy, my job, my prosperity, and Your gifts and anointing. I loosen all that satan has hindered sevenfold, 1, 2, 3, 4, 5, 6, 7 times, by the power of the Holy Spirit, in the name of the Lord Jesus Christ. Amen.

*"DAY 3 - BRINGING BACK ALL THAT WAS TAKEN*

*Scripture Reference;*

>>Mathew 15:10-11 10 And he called the multitude, and said unto them, Hear, and understand:  11 Not that which goeth into the mouth defileth a man; but that which cometh out of the mouth, this defileth a man.

>>Joel 1:17-27 17 Let the priests, the ministers of the Lord, weep

between the porch and the altar, and let them say, spare thy people, O Lord, and give not thine heritage to reproach, that the heathen should rule over them: wherefore should they say among the people, where is their God?  18 Then will the Lord be jealous for his land, and pity his people.  19 Yea, the Lord will answer and say unto his people, Behold, I will send you corn, and wine, and oil, and ye shall be satisfied therewith: and I will no more make you a reproach among the heathen:  20 But I will remove far off from you the northern army, and will drive him into a land barren and desolate, with his face toward the east sea, and his hinder part toward the utmost sea, and his stink shall come up, and his ill savour shall come up because he hath done great things.  21 Fear not, O land; be glad and rejoice: for the Lord will do great things.  22 Be not afraid, ye beasts of the field: for the pastures of the wilderness do spring, for the tree beareth her fruit, the fig tree and the vine do yield their strength.  23 Be glad then, ye children of Zion, and rejoice in the Lord your God: for he hath given you the former rain moderately, and he will cause to come down for you the rain, the former rain, and the latter rain in the first month.  24 And the floors shall be full of wheat, and the fats shall overflow with wine and oil.  25 And I will restore to you the years that the locust hath eaten, the cankerworm, and the caterpillar, and the palmer worm, my great army which I sent among you.  26 And ye shall eat in plenty, and be satisfied, and praise the name of the Lord your God, that hath dealt wondrously with you: and my people shall never be ashamed.  27 And ye shall know that I am in the midst of Israel, and that I am the Lord your God, and none else: and my people shall never be ashamed.

>>Mathew 15:13 But he answered and said, every plant, which my heavenly Father hath not planted, shall be rooted up.

Begin by expressing gratitude to God, for it is not what enters you that defiles, but what comes out of your mouth, as stated in Matthew 15:10-11. Position yourself in Matthew 15:13 and petition God to remove everything He did not plant within you. Request that the Lord restore the years you have lost—years spent unemployed, ill, single, or incarcerated. Refer to Joel 1:17-27 and ask God to reclaim the years seized by your adversaries. Entreat the Lord to send rain that will nurture all your crops. Stand on Joel 2:23 and implore God to make your crops flourish in the first month of the harvest. For Joel 2:23 declares: "Be joyful, people of Zion, and rejoice in the Lord your God, for He has granted you the autumn rains in faithfulness. He sends you plentiful showers, both autumn and spring rains, as before."

Concluding your prayers by seeking signs from the Lord is a practice of faith. When referring to signs, typically, there are three types that one may receive. These signs can manifest through dreams, visions, or tangible occurrences related to your prayers. It is crucial to pray for God's mercy to ensure that when these signs appear, you have the wisdom to interpret them correctly.

*DAY 4 - WORSHIP, OFFER PRAISE AND THANKSGIVING THROUGH THESE VERSES.*

*Scripture Reference*

>>Psalms 133 1 How good and pleasant it is when God's people live together in unity! 2 It is like precious oil poured on the head, running down on the beard, running down on Aaron's beard, down on the collar of his robe. 3 It is as if the dew of Hermon were falling on Mount Zion. For there the Lord bestows his blessing, even life forevermore.

>>Psalms 134 1 Praise the Lord, all you servants of the Lord who minister by night in the house of the Lord. 2 Lift up your hands in the sanctuary and praise the Lord. 3 May the Lord bless you from Zion, he who is the Maker of heaven and earth.

>>Psalms 135 1 Praise the Lord. Praise the name of the Lord; praise him, you servants of the Lord, 2 you who minister in the house of the Lord, in the courts of the house of our God. 3 Praise the Lord, for the Lord is good; sing praise to his name, for that is pleasant. 4 For the Lord has chosen Jacob to be his own, Israel to be his treasured possession. 5 I know that the Lord is great, that our Lord is greater than all God's. 6 The Lord does whatever pleases him, in the heavens and on the earth, in the seas and all their depths. 7 He makes clouds rise from the ends of the earth; he sends lightning with the rain and brings out the wind from his storehouses. 8 He struck down the first born of Egypt, the first born of people and animals. 9 He sent his signs and wonders into your midst, Egypt, against Pharaoh and all his servants. 10 He struck down many

nations and killed mighty kings— 11 Sihon king of the Amorites, Og king of Bashan, and all the kings of Canaan. 12 and he gave their land as an inheritance, an inheritance to his people Israel. 13 Your name, Lord, endures forever, your renown, Lord, through all generations. 14 For the Lord will vindicate his people and have compassion on his servants.15 The idols of the nations are silver and gold, made by human hands. 16 They have mouths, but cannot speak, eyes, but cannot see. 17 They have ears, but cannot hear, nor is there breath in their mouths. 18 Those who make them will be like them, and so will all who trust in them. 19 All you Israelites, praise the Lord; house of Aaron, praise the Lord; 20 house of Levi, praise the Lord; you who fear him, praise the Lord. 21 Praise be to the Lord from Zion, to him who dwells in Jerusalem.

# PRAISE THE LORD.

On the fourth day, all those three psalms should be recited one after the other, seven times each.

# Lesson Nineteen

# YOU ARE GOING TO DIE

Your mission on Earth is to share the gospel.
This gospel you are to preach aims to light up the
darkness in the world. Many have perished because of
this gospel. People will despise you, for the gospel you
proclaim is the truth and it exposes the evil within them.

Life is likened to a sailing boat on a voyage to heaven, and it is not always a pleasant journey. Jesus told his disciples that they were not seeing the bigger picture; they would face persecution for his sake. This larger perspective has persisted since he spoke those words and will continue until the end. Followers of the Lord will be despised and persecuted just as he was, for speaking the truth to the world. Through his followers, he continues to speak. The world, engulfed in sin, needs awakening through you. Sin has proliferated and found acceptance through concepts like human rights. Scriptures are often ridiculed as archaic, with rules deemed irrelevant for modern times. The question arises: do people still believe in a divine presence governing the world? Only a few hold this belief, and they are seen as hindrances to what many consider liberation from accountability.

Most preachers have been asked about homosexuality and they can't find a position to deny the act. Stating that stealing is wrong does not imply that a thief ought to be killed. The truth, stealing is bad. Homosexuality is bad, you have not judged a homosexual. How effective can you be in assisting smokers to quit if you avoid discussing the consequences of smoking? In the end, you are killing them. Your God instructed you to speak it loud for the sinner to know or else you will be judged like him. But now you are scared to talk about sin. You are scared to teach about sin as written in the scriptures for fear of persecution from these sinners. This is how far man has let the devil go free. You should not be scared to talk about sin. Homosexuality is a sin. The origin of sin is satan, and the origin of homosexuality is satan.

It is essential to educate the world about the perfect creation of man. This understanding extends to animals as well. Homosexuality are spirits, and some of the strongest spirits next to promiscuous. Teach the world to know that this spirit can be fought. There is nothing like being born in a man's body. I reiterate, "90% of our actions and words are influenced by the spiritual world." Homosexuality is an evil influence from the spiritual world. We should not hesitate to proclaim the truth to the world. Accepting the Lord Jesus Christ shifts our hope from this life to the next. Death is merely a transition, a journey we all must embark on. Do not allow fear of death to deter you from the truth. The world may despise you, and you may face persecution for your faith in Jesus Christ. You may walk a path marked by disgrace, but within your heart, there is joy, for you are assured that He who is within you governs the future and accompanies you.

# Lesson Twenty

## HELL IS FOR SATAN

satan has faced judgment, and redemption is not his
to claim. Yet he declares, "Even those you cherish will
transgress as I have." He yearns for man to share in his
sin, for man is cherished by God. Nonetheless, man is not
destined to tread satan's path. They should shun hell, for
it is the abode designated for satan.

One day, a man shared his testimony. He claimed that in a past life, he had been a witch. He went by the name Pastor Ssebukyu. During his time practicing witchcraft, he would sing songs that were believed to summon evil spirits. One such song was interpreted to mean "fire burns from top to bottom."

Indeed, it is acknowledged that the devil is aware of the divine wrath. The scriptures, particularly the words of the Lord Jesus Christ, reveal the devil's intentions on Earth. The prophet Isaiah provides insights into the conflict between the devil and God's ultimate plan for him. The devil, being more than a mere mortal, understands the nature of God and the significance of divine judgment. The pronouncements made by the Lord Jesus Christ regarding the devil in the Gospels, as well as the prophecies detailed in Revelation, are immutable and will come to pass. The devil is cognizant of his predetermined doom and awaits the execution of the judgment rendered. Repentance is not within his capacity, and it would be futile even if it were. satan challenges the Lord, claiming that even those who you believe in will falter. This refers to all humanity on Earth. The devil has deviated from his original purpose and now seeks to lead humanity astray with profane practices. However, with the grace of the Lord, one need not follow such paths. Disobeying the commands of God serves no purpose, especially not for the sake of transient, earthly gains.

The quest to redeem humanity began well before humans were created. The patriarchs through whom God initiated this mission were unaware of the battles they were part of. Abraham did not realize his faith was a step in the journey of mankind's salvation. Likewise, when Moses penned the words of the Lord, he could not  foresee the divine plans those words entailed. Reading the Exodus, the Promised Land seems like the journey's conclusion, but it was, in fact, just the start. Many prophecies about the arrival of the Lord Jesus Christ were made in the Promised Land (Israel), and these promises, among others, will endure until the world's end. The devil is aware of this and strives to undermine your faith. The scriptures depict the Lord Jesus expressing the joy of salvation: "In the same way, I tell you, there is rejoicing in the presence of the angels of God over one sinner who repents."

It is a struggle for a person to make decisions in life, and even more so to make the right ones. Surrounded by the hatred of fallen angels who despise God, they persist in trying to sway your feelings against the Lord your God. It is a profound miracle that you, a person who has never seen God's face, have chosen to praise, worship, and find faith in Him. The devil, who knew God's face, power, and splendor, chose to revolt. It is a tremendous honor that you have believed without seeing. Imagine, then, the magnificence awaiting in heaven when you behold the Glory of the Lord.

From the outset, God dispatched His servants to caution His people about Hellfire. God Himself arrived to reinforce this warning. It is only through Him that one can be spared from this fire. This fire should be left to the devil, for whom it was originally intended. The devil desires for you to emulate him. The scriptures state clearly, "The thief comes only to steal, kill, and destroy." The thief wants humanity to engage in theft, murder, and destruction. Ultimately, the devil's aim is to turn you away from your God, to partake in his punishment. He aspires to lead many into darkness, believing this will compel the Heavenly Father to revoke his sentence. He thinks if all humanity and the angels in Heaven oppose the Father, his rebellion will be justified. However, God is just, and therefore He declares, "I came that they may have life, and have it abundantly." Place your trust in the Lord, and you shall consign the fire to the devil, for whom it was created.

# Lesson Twenty One

## JUST BELIEVE

What drives a man to leave his familiar homeland in search of unknown lands on the strength of a promise? What motivated the men in the scriptures to take the actions they did? It was their faith in God. The scriptures stand as testimony to God's existence. Faith is the essential element to understanding their deep truths.

The scriptures are replete with tales of righteous men who remained steadfast on God's path until the end. It may seem straightforward to stay true to God's path amidst temptations when reading scripture. However, interpreting these men's lives reveals not just their faithfulness but their complete devotion to the Lord, both in body and spirit. What drives a man to leave his ancestral land for an unknown territory based on a promise? What compels a man to construct an ark based on faith in things unseen? What instills in you the hope in the Lord Jesus Christ and the conviction that the teachings of men you've never encountered in the scriptures are indeed the truth?

Many debates about the scriptures focus on their veracity. People have traveled to Egypt and Israel in search of scriptural truths. Some assert that Jesus was black, citing tests in South Africa that show similarities to the Israelites of Jesus' era. The quest for truth through history has often involved both sight and intellect. It raises the question of why there is a preoccupation with Jesus' race—whether he was white or black, or even if it would matter if he were blue. The pursuit has shifted from salvation to proving existence, with all disputes centering on the authenticity of the scriptures and, fundamentally, the existence of God.

My friends, children of God, I am here to affirm that the Lord God indeed exists. The secret you failed; the purpose of the scriptures is not merely to recount admirable stories about the Lord but to serve as a roadmap to finding Him. It's not about discovering Him after death, but rather walking with Him on this earth and being with Him after life.

I am writing to affirm that the Lord exists and is present on this earth. This message is to help everyone comprehend that God is real, and by adhering to His teachings, you will undoubtedly encounter Him. The scriptures recount how prophets like Ezekiel, Isaiah, Samuel, and Elijah communicated with the Lord. Through their deeds, they were in God's company, and it was through them that the Lord's message was conveyed to the world.

Throughout my life, I have walked the earth as any man, living ordinarily. Yet, I have always been accompanied by the Spirit of the Lord. Initially, I believed His presence when I heard His voice. Now, I realize that He has been with me all along. I didn't learn about the scriptures in a convent; I was just an ordinary person, living a daily life. However, I had an unrecognized calling. I led my life and acted on my own understanding until the day the Lord revealed Himself to me, transforming my mindset. I no longer attribute waking up to my own strength. I witness marvels that I cannot express to the world. He has instructed me and fortified my belief in Him. I do not fear death, nor do I fear offending you with my words. He has instilled in me a faith that since His arrival, my actions are not for myself, but for Him. He guides my words, deeds, and even as I write this. Therefore, I proclaim to everyone, God is alive and dwells among His people.

The life I have led is the life of a man, to show that nothing God has ordained is too difficult for man. I have endured the life and temptations of man, yet I continue to walk in the Lord's light. You have simply not found the path to God. Your hearts are too tainted to hear His voice. You are envious of those who know His whereabouts and you judge them for their gifts. "Can anything good come out of Nazareth? Can anything good come from the poor?" You have judged those who are with the Lord and failed to see that the Lord humbles His servants. I write persistently so that you may understand. My writings are not for me, but for all who seek the Lord's spirit. Through my words, I hope you recognize that these are not the meditations of a mere man. Through my writing, I wish for you to recognize that the Lord is within me, and through me, He urges the world to turn away from sin.

# Lesson Twenty Two

# INTERCESSION

Who qualifies as an intercessor, and does this role extend to all members of the church? Furthermore, as an intercessor, are you clear on the expectations placed upon you  by  God in this capacity?

Intercession is often misunderstood within the church. An intercessor is not just anyone; it is a role endowed by the Holy Spirit . The scriptures say, "I searched for someone among them who could build up the wall and stand before me in the gap on behalf of the land so I would not have to destroy it, but I found no one."

Not everyone is called to intercede. Many figures in the scriptures, including our Lord Jesus Christ, served as intercessors. Today, the Holy Spirit  is considered the most powerful intercessor. Church intercessors should  not  be  just anyone who volunteers; they should be individuals who possess this gift from the Holy Spirit . Those who are truly gifted by God cannot remain hidden; through His mercy, the Lord communicates and acts through them, allowing their gifts to be recognized and acknowledged by many.

An intercessor stands in the gap, taking the place of the sinner. On behalf of humanity, the Lord Jesus Christ bore the shame. He endured the pain, shed the tears, and accepted death. This is the role of an intercessor, bridging the gap for the sinner.

There is a tale of a man who served as an intercessor. His friend confided in him about his father's illness, which the intercessor perceived as a spiritual attack. Upon agreeing to pray for the ailing father, he himself was besieged by evil spirits. He experienced such intense chest pain that he was rendered speechless and devoid of strength. After his prayer, he recounted his ordeal to the friend's father, who replied, "My son, you understand precisely what I feel." Such is the nature of intercession.

You take the place of the sinner. Nehemiah took the place of Israel; Jesus took the place of man. He did not blame man for their sins but expressed gratitude to the Father for the ability to stand in their place. This is reserved for those who receive God's mercy. Before his death, Jesus Christ bore pain on behalf of man. He rejoiced in his choice to intercede, for through it, man gained life. Rejoice in interceding for others. Recognize that sin entered in man, but man is not the sin. As God's image on earth, represent Him as He truly deserves. Intercession means standing in for the sinner or the sin itself. Ezekiel interceded for Israel, even when Israel was unaware of his intercession. The Lord instructed Ezekiel, "Also lie on your left side, and place the iniquity of the house of Israel upon it. For the number of days you lie on it, you will bear their iniquity."

An intercessor, chosen by God, possesses a pure heart, speaking only truth. This intercessor embraces sin without blaming the sinner, embodying the sin on behalf of others. His life and heart are devoted to the sin he stands in for. An intercessor's persistence endures until change occurs, becoming bound to the cause he pleads for. He persists in prayer until he receives a response, as the angel told Daniel, "Your prayers were heard from the beginning, but the prince of Persia hindered me until Michael the Archangel intervened." Daniel's persistence was key.

# Lesson Twenty Three

## YOU ARE THE SINNER'S HOPE TO HEAVEN

Not everyone on Earth is familiar with the concept of a heavenly Father. Throughout different cultures, various deities are  worshiped, with followers convinced of their legitimacy. Take for instance adherents of Islam, Buddhism, and other faiths who do not recognize the God of Israel. Nevertheless, you are aware of the true God of Israel. You stand as the only ray of hope  for these people to achieve salvation.

How many of you recognize the privilege of being saved? Claiming it as the best decision you made isn't entirely in one's hands; how does one make such a choice? No one comes to the Lord unless the father draws him. Reflect on your childhood and youth, the times spent in church observing men and women in tears during worship and prayer. The question that arose within yourself was simple: Do they believe in God's existence? Why do they cry for someone unseen? This curiosity turned into a prayer, a yearning for tangible proof of God's existence. It's hard to believe, but it was indeed a powerful prayer. Once that prayer is answered, all other earthly needs seem insignificant.

Consider the less fortunate brothers and sisters wandering the streets daily, unaware of who God is. They've heard of the Lord Jesus Christ, yet they question one thing: does He truly exist? They go about their days unconcerned about the future, oblivious to the concept of sin. Yet, without the Lord Jesus Christ, one is in sin. What they fail to recognize is that satan influences every decision they make.

You are fortunate to know God, for you feel His presence when you call His name. You can remain steadfast through persecution, proclaiming your knowledge of Him. Now is the time to ask God for his mercy, so the world may understand who he is. This is a mercy He will always grant, for He sacrificed Himself for this purpose. Your mission is to be a fisher of men, to reach out to those held captive by darkness on the streets. You may be their sole path to the glory of the Lord.

# Lesson Twenty Four

# POUR SALT ALL AROUND THE INSIDE WALLS

God continues to fight man's battles as He did in the times recorded in the scriptures. Just as He fought alongside Moses, He battled with Elisha. He will engage in the same battle for you today.

The scriptures recount that he proceeded to the spring of waters, threw salt into it, and declared, "thus says the Lord, 'I have healed these waters; henceforth, there shall be no more death or barrenness.'"

The signs of spiritual attacks are not always detectable. You need to believe that all man, faithful to Christ, experience spiritual attacks on a daily basis. Often, these attacks are said to manifest in various ways. It's true that those with little faith may not comprehend their meaning, while those who are blessed with God's mercy recognize them when they occur and understand they are under spiritual attack.

As you mature in faith and gain a deeper understanding of the spiritual world, there are signs you should not overlook. Do not dismiss the appearance of a snail in your home, or a frog on a chair, especially when you do not live near a swamp. There is no reason for rats and mice to be in your house. When you notice them, immediate action is necessary. Your lack of understanding of the Lord your God has led to a misunderstanding of these signs. Consequently, when you face spiritual attacks, you may be uncertain of how to handle them.

The scriptures describe Elisha as being filled with the spirit of the Lord, which gave him profound insight into the spiritual realm. This insight goes beyond simply learning and reciting a song; it involves participating in spiritual warfare, each battle fought in a unique way as directed by the Holy Spirit . It is noted, "he went to the source of the waters, threw salt into it, and proclaimed, 'thus says the Lord: I have purified these waters;

there shall no longer be any death or barrenness from them.'" Elisha utilized salt to cleanse the waters, revitalizing the previously infertile land. In a similar account, the scriptures narrate Moses' experience: "Moses pleaded with the Lord, who then showed him a piece of wood. He cast it into the waters, and they turned sweet. There, the Lord set forth a statute and a law, and there he tested them."

These scriptures illustrate the various methods God employed to address identical issues. However, the crucial point is that both Moses and Elisha were anointed by God, able to hear from and communicate with the Lord. Although Moses and Elisha are gone, similar challenges persist. The uplifting truth is that the Lord our God remains. The Lord God still enacts miracles and, through his servants, continues to work wonders in the world.

One morning, a man awoke to find ants swarming the interior of his bedroom. The ants had devoured the walls, leaving the edges filled with soil. In distress, he called out to the Lord about the calamity in his home. The Lord replied, "you are under spiritual attack." He was instructed by the Lord to spread salt along the interior walls of his house, ensuring no wall was left unsalted. Once every wall was lined with salt, he was to exit to the main entrance of his house and draw a cross with anointing oil at the doorway, invoking the name of the father, the son, and the Holy Spirit . He was to pray and decree, "let everything in this house that does not come from God leave through this cross." The salt was to remain for seven days. He obeyed the Lord's instructions, salting the interior wall edges and drawing the cross at the entrance. He declared that all malevolence within his home should depart via the cross. Within a day, the ants had disappeared even though the salt was supposed to remain in the house for seven days.

Pray and heed the Lord, for he is real. He speaks and will guide you through life's challenges. He made a promise, and he is here to wage your wars. Just as he did for the prophets, he does so today. The same struggles faced by the prophets persist now. You are the prophets, and he will combat your struggles as he has in the past.

# Lesson Twenty Five

## ONLY GOD KNOWS

**The most difficult journey any man will walk is a journey of knowing what the world does not know.
For what the world does not know, the world will never believe. This journey is the journey the Lord Jesus walked on this earth.**

I cannot speak extensively about your experiences on the path to salvation, particularly for those who have been institutionalized in mental hospitals. The teachings in this book present a formidable challenge, as they pertain to a spiritual war—wars of such a nature are complex and not easily elucidated. As your faith deepens, you may encounter discussions about individuals deemed insane following their rebirth in faith. You may wonder, how can one descend into madness after placing belief in the giver of life?

In a mental hospital, the confusion is palpable. Many believe you are mentally ill because you have been 'born again.' However, you concur that it's an ordeal no one should endure. Should you ever find yourself in a mental hospital, you might wonder how one could escape such an experience. A man, forcibly admitted, recounts, "I had no friends in that hospital. I was constantly bombarded with voices delivering incessant, erroneous messages that I couldn't silence. The people around me never had faith in me; to them, I was merely a patient in uniform. They appeared to understand when I spoke, yet I could discern their true thoughts. Their unanimous verdict was clear: 'He is insane.'"

The most challenging thing in this world is to possess knowledge that has never been known, with no adequate means to explain it. This becomes even more perplexing when it pertains to God. It's crucial to recognize that while scriptures contain much information, there's still a great deal that remains unwritten. Consider spiritual wars; aside from the brief account of Job, what else is known about such conflicts? The scriptures recount the Lord, in his final days, asking for the burden of battle to be lifted from him. Such a struggle can only truly be comprehended by those who have endured it.

Jesus said to Nicodemus, "Truly, we speak of what we know and testify to what we have seen, yet you do not accept our testimony." In the mental hospital, the man was a captive, a spiritual prisoner encircled by evil spirits. This was not an error; it was preordained. Upon his release, to the astonishment of many, including his family, no one was pleased. No one grasped the events that had unfolded in his life. After being freed, nobody approached him or inquired about his experiences, though he held the answers and could have elucidated the transgressions that had befallen his life.

Now he is liberated. His time of temptation has passed, and what was revealed to him in that period holds greater value for his future as a devotee of God. He need not struggle for the world's recognition of his identity or his transformation, for God understands how He shapes His faithful. Moses once killed an Egyptian and never regained his royal stature, but God charted a course of growth for Moses—a path that would honor the Lord's name. The journey you read about in this book is the one the Lord has chosen for this man, to manifest His glory on earth and in the heavens. The Lord, omniscient and all-preparing, anticipates the future. He perceives the hearts of men and the frailties the devil exploits to sow doubt among God's children.

I have walked among you in the flesh, living as you do in this world. Let no one claim, "I cannot remain faithful to the Lord and lead a devout life in this world." This world is under the Father's dominion, and you are His beloved offspring. He has revealed Himself to demonstrate the magnitude of His love for humanity. To show that the life you lead is one ordained by the Lord, a life that can be victorious. This life paves the way to the God of love, against whom no force on earth or in heaven can prevail. And no individual should hesitate to exalt the Lord their God, out of fear of any earthly or celestial power, for the Lord God governs all in both realms.

# Lesson Twenty Six

# YOUR MIRACLE, IS THE LORD HIMSELF

**Moving from one church to another in search of a miracle overlooks a vital lesson – miracles are indications of God's presence. The most significant miracle you possess is within you, and that is the presence of the Lord Jesus Christ.**

When was the last time you offered a testimony? It should be a daily practice, especially to oneself. Often, this will also be heard by the devil, who is always listening. Opportunities to share a testimony in church may be rare, but there are countless testimonies that reside within your heart, and God is aware of them. The good works God has performed in you are the reason for your love for Him. Good works aren't just miraculous healings, like gaining sight after blindness; they are the recognition that your journey thus far could only have been possible with God's guidance.

Many seek to pray and experience the Holy Spirit's presence. Yet, how many can truly sense that presence without witnessing a physical miracle? This is what Jesus refers to as God's mercy. The scriptures say, "They will pick up snakes with their hands; and if they drink any deadly poison, it will not hurt them; they will lay hands on the sick, and they will recover." Look for the signs of God's presence, which often shine brightly within you. Recognizing these signs will enrich your walk with God.

A man of God was journeying through a city when he encountered an elderly woman, clad in tattered rags. The Lord God instructed him, "Take what you have in your pocket and give it to this woman." Unaware of the man's divine connection, the old woman declined the offering, asserting, "I am fine, and I don't need assistance." Later, the Lord revealed to His servant, "There was a purpose for you to offer her that gift. One day she will realize that I was present. The offering she dismissed came from Me, her God." The gift she refused was God Himself. Her eyes were too veiled to recognize God's benevolence. Her miracle arrived on a path unknown to her, delivered by a man she had never met before.

Not every time will you witness a burning bush as Moses did, or be surrounded by tongues of fire like the disciples. God manifests Himself to His faithful in diverse ways. For Moses, it was fire; for Jacob, it was Rachel; for the disciples, it was Pentecost; and for Paul, it was blindness. What is your experience? God operates in modest events. The Lord Jesus Christ walked in humility, which the world never expected from its God. God moves upon this earth and is always among His people. Yet, many push Him aside for the love of power and wealth, for He appears less than what they desire.

Offer a testimony to fortify yourself and fellow believers in Christ who listen to your words. Share testimonies so the world may recognize the lengths to which the Lord will go for His people. When you pray or worship, let your testimony be heard, for even the adversary listens. Proclaim testimonies to remind the adversary of the One who dwells within you. He is aware and acknowledges the might of your God. He may challenge the goodness within you, but remember, you are never alone. The Holy Spirit will hold you near and remind you of the One who resides in you. This is the wonder for which you should contend. Manifest the Lord's presence to those who are yet to grasp His ways and are novices on this path. Many have not recognized the Lord because they rely on sight, yet they lack the vision to perceive. Truly knowing the Lord transcends what you see and feel; it is about what resides within you.

For the Lord Jesus Christ has made a promise: "And I will ask the Father, and He will give you another advocate to help you and be with you forever—the Spirit of truth. The world cannot accept Him because it neither sees Him nor knows Him. But you know Him, for He lives with you and will be in you." The Spirit of the Lord is within me, and I am a testimony to all. I do not just feel Him or see Him, but I have become one with Him.

## GIVE PRAISE TO THE LORD WITH YOUR WHOLE HEART.

# Lesson Twenty Seven

## YOU HAVE TO WAIT

I understand that you pray multiple times a day out of love for the Lord God, adhere to a fasting schedule, and attend church every Sunday. Even so, you might not have yet seen the results of your prayers. My encouragement to you is to simply wait.

I address you, the faithful disciples of the Lord Jesus Christ, who have prayed diligently yet witnessed no breakthrough. You may serve in the church and often fast, but it appears that within your circle, you are the one who has not succeeded.

This mirrors the lives of many. They feel forsaken, praying and worshipping daily, yet their prayers seem unanswered. Meanwhile, those around them appear to receive everything they ask for. To those losing hope, I want to instill confidence. The Scriptures remind us, "There are still four months until the harvest," "but I say, look at the fields, they are ready for harvest". The Lord your God is your most precious gift, present in times of waiting and in times of abundance. Rejoice in your current trials, for remember, all who have attained greatness through the Lord have walked this very path.

Every man who has received glory through the Lord's intervention has endured a period of waiting. Moses spent years in anticipation before and after the burning bush incident before he approached Pharaoh at the age of 80 to advocate for the Lord's people. Similarly, Joseph was brought to Egypt at the age of 17 and did not ascend to the role of governor until his 30s. These events illustrate that the time leading up to their divinely appointed roles was a period of preparation.

Moses killed an Egyptian guard to defend an Israelite and was destined to lead and safeguard God's people for the remainder of his life. Joseph appeared to be a failure, enduring hardship at the hands of his brothers. Wrongly accused of rape by his master's wife, he was imprisoned. Yet, these trials set the stage for his rise to the governorship of Egypt, a role few realized would pave the way for the establishment of the sacred nation of Israel, through which God would bring salvation to man.

I recognize the feeling of being the only one who appears to have failed. I've seen girls grow up in the church and become women. They join the youth choir and eventually leave, yet they stay single. Many switch churches, seeking marriage, but it never materializes. I've seen someone commit to the Lord Jesus Christ, only to lose their job months later. They've been unemployed for nearly three years, their housing paid for by their sister—a hefty sum each month. Their mother provides weekly sustenance and care. Indeed, it's a period of trial. Nevertheless, one must persist in hope, believing that God will raise them up again. Your clothes will wear out, everything you buy will break down, and there may come a time when you can't afford replacements. Even for a simple journey that was once affordable, you may have to walk. You are not merely waiting; no one has the strength to wait in such a tempting life. Many would succumb to the levels of wanting to kill themselves, but not you, for you are with God. During these years of hardship, you will come to know God's goodness. It is then that you will feel the Holy Spirit, receive all His gifts, and gain understanding. These will also be the years when you will face the toughest battles.

You may lose everything around you, but never lose hope. Never lose faith in God, for He is all you have, and at the end, whether rich or poor, He will remain. In the years you lack, you may become a burden to many. Your family may request that you return home to save on rent. The Lord will provide for you, and along the many unknown paths, you will receive everything you need. Just like the prophet Elijah, who was provided for through the widow, you'll have all that you need. Rest assured that God will take care of you until the time comes for your harvest. Stay strong and have faith, especially now that you are in need. Trust in everything that is unfolding in your life. This journey and path have been ordained by the Lord for you, so that your victories are not a return to the past but a means to empower others.

# Lesson Twenty Eight

## PERSIST WITH THE LORD

I write to encourage you as you face the challenges on your Christian path. In a world full of temptations, you might feel weak and unsure about staying on the right track. Remember, you are not alone; you will reach your goal. Just like those who have triumphed before you, you will succeed. Keep pushing forward.

This message is for you, the Christian enduring suffering. You who are engaged in a struggle that only you can comprehend. None of those around you grasp the extent of what you endure. You stand with many Christians, the devout followers of Jesus Christ, who face the devil's temptations, yet find their experiences met with disbelief. You are assailed by dark spirits, and not even those in your prayer circle can fathom your battle.

In this book, I have written about various temptations, including the experiences of those admitted to mental hospitals, to fortify you in the name of our Lord Jesus Christ. Often, it is through temptations that we learn about our struggles and gain strength. Consider a well-known preacher who abandoned his wife for another woman. Previously, he had dismissed the value of a wedding ring for a Christian and had even proclaimed his intent to burn most Bibles, claiming the Word of God had been altered in those texts. These are among the many accusations leveled against him. However, such behaviors may indicate a man undergoing a period of temptation. If he recognizes and understands this path and remains true to the Lord Jesus Christ, he will overcome this battle and emerge transformed. As the scriptures say: "No man, when he hath lighted a candle, covereth it with a vessel, or putteth it under a bed; but setteth it on a candlestick, that they which enter in may see the light."

Many church leaders have committed evil acts against God, yet God assures us that we will recognize them. When He illuminates the darkness, their misdeeds will be exposed. Peter faced the same temptations as Judas. However, Peter overcame his trials and continued to follow the Lord until his death. The Lord Jesus said to Simon Peter, "Simon, satan has asked to sift you as wheat, but I have prayed for you so that your faith will not falter; and once you have recovered, you are to strengthen your brothers." Peter's temptation served as preparation for his future responsibilities. His situation echoes that of Job, whom the devil sought to dismantle. This pattern did not end with Job but continued with Peter and persists to this day. The devil is ever eager to shatter your faith in the Lord, aiming to demonstrate your unworthiness. Yet, you are not here by accident; the Lord is aware of your path and assures that your faith shall not falter. As many embark on this journey, one might wonder, what is God's purpose for your path?

Peter served as the foundation for the growth of the Lord's word. The Lord Jesus Christ proclaimed, "Once you have turned back, strengthen your brethren." God may allow temptations to fortify you for your destiny. The Spirit led Jesus into the wilderness to be tempted. Peter was transformed following his temptation. A man who overcomes such trials emerges with profound knowledge and strength to fortify others. These trials are the work of the devil, who is keen to demonstrate that no child of God can withstand him and remain distinct from his nature.

This message is for the Christian enduring temptations as a means to fortify their faith in the Lord. Many followers of Christ may not recognize that their trials are part of this journey of temptations until it concludes. Yet, every person on earth traverses this path. From the moment you dedicated your life to Jesus Christ, your life became a testament to all who faltered before. Sin embodies satan, and no one can traverse this world in righteousness without battling sin. If you are chosen, like Peter, to illuminate the path for others, expect a challenging journey strewn with obstacles. Your resolve must be to remain in the light, for God accompanies you. Every temptation you face is not with your strength alone, but with the strength of the One who guided you onto this path. He is with you and will remain so until the end. Stay strong, for this journey is yours, and only four moons remain until the harvest. On the day a man was discharged from the mental hospital, he remained unchanged from what they claimed was his ailment. He continued to speak in tongues and pray in many languages. Yet, he walked through the hospital gates a liberated man. The guards who had beaten him on various occasions now waved, calling out his name in astonishment. It was over; he had triumphed.

I can speak about the Lord's work fearlessly because I am well-versed in it. Many have navigated through this life filled with temptations. Often, these trials are placed by God Himself to strengthen you. Through these challenges, you come to understand satan and are thus prepared to uphold God's kingdom on earth, undaunted by darkness. If He was with you and through Him, you overcame the darkness, then what power does the darkness have to obstruct your path? You possess the weapon, and that weapon is God's mercy.

# Lesson Twenty Nine

## YOU ARE ISRAEL

The scriptures recount the stories of Israel, Moses, Jacob, Isaac, and Abraham, through whom God spoke and performed wonders. All that is documented in the Holy Scriptures represents His deeds. These acts were carried out for your benefit. You are not an accident; you were intentionally created. Seek God's attention through those He has worked through. The deeds He accomplished through them, He can also accomplish through you.

What motivates you to keep going despite facing persecution? Just yesterday one of the biggest books selling company is to stop selling books that speak wrong about homosexuality. It's the followers of Christ that rebuke the act of homosexuality. What this bookseller met was, that he would not sell any Christian books. The world has been turned against the Lord Jesus Christ by the devil, a circumstance not exclusive to modern times but also evident during Jesus's earthly life. Knowing that even those closest to him were reluctant to continue, Jesus recognized his impending solitude, stating, "I will be alone."

Where God resides, the devil also exists. Where goodness is found, evil is also present. Jesus informed his disciples that one among them was the devil. He commanded satan to get behind him, safeguarding Peter from the devil's malign influence. Addressing Judas, the Lord spoke not to the man, but to the devil who had completely taken hold of him, saying, "What you are about to do, do quickly." This is the teaching I have shared before. It is important to recognize that your actions are influenced by the spiritual world.

In this world, you do not battle alone but are influenced by other forces. Worship and prayer to the Lord are only possible through the Holy Spirit. There will be times when prayer becomes a struggle. The devil is aware of your prayer schedule, such as your 9:00 pm daily prayer, and you may miss this appointed time. However, the Holy Spirit often prompts you to pray earlier, as your adversaries may learn your prayer times and attempt to thwart you before you can pray. The spiritual world is indeed a battlefield, one in which you are engaged, often without your knowledge.

When adversaries resort to witchcraft, their initial attempts may fail. Upon failure, they seek guidance from evil spirits. These spirits advise them to alter the timing of their attacks. Consequently, you notice an increase in the frequency of these attacks compared to before.

Do not underestimate the power of darkness. By underestimating the devil, he gains the opportunity to erode God's kingdom within the hearts of people. Cult worshippers operate in the shadows, and while we may believe they are nonexistent, they are indeed present. They have corrupted the world with wealth and shaped what is heard by the masses, leaving us, the people of God, voiceless.

God is the creator of this world and a jealous God. He will accompany you through this struggle, and the world will recognize His presence. Despite the world's regression into disbelief over thousands of years, the same God remains. Your faith is your sustenance amidst persecution. Remain on the narrow path that leads to life. While the world may stray from God, you shall not. It is your duty to guide the world back to God, a battle every person should engage in with pride. Rise and speak out against hate and the threat of death. The world must be informed about the Lord your God. Jeremiah stood and spoke among the formidable men of his era. He alone believed in his words. Yet, the Lord God stood by him, and when His words were fulfilled, the Lord's name was exalted.

Fearing sinners makes you similar to them, for you become what you fear to confront. The world must be shown the goodness of our God, and you possess the knowledge to do so. Seek God's mercy, and it shall be granted to you. Proclaim that you are the Moses, the Jacob, the David, the Peter, and the Paul of today. While these great men of God no longer walk this earth, you do. Pray for the Lord's protection and for the wisdom to disseminate His holy name.

## YOU PRAY

Heavenly Father, I seek Your mercy on this journey. Amidst persecution, grant me strength and the power to adhere to Your word. You cherished Abraham, yet he is no longer here. You honored Jacob, bestowing upon him the name Israel for Your great nation, yet he is no longer here. You accompanied David, exalted Solomon, and uplifted Peter, yet they are no longer here. Heavenly Father, now, in this moment and in this life, I stand to carry Your word forward. Bestow upon me Your mercy to uphold Your image and combat the evil in this world. Deliver Your word to those who sin, that they may transform. Guide me in this struggle and fortify me when I am weak. I pray, by the power of the Holy Spirit, in the name of Jesus Christ, Amen.

<h1 style="text-align:center">Lesson Thirty</h1>

# THE LIFE-GIVING WATER

You might search for all the wealth in the world, yet you won't find the happiness you're seeking, as the world often gives with resentment.  The Lord Jesus Christ is the water you need, beyond which you need not search.

ou may feel depressed, become sad, and often struggle to move forward. Your day may be ruined repeatedly, and you might find yourself blaming the Lord for these failures. Often, you may find it hard to express worship. You believe in your heart that it's all because the Lord didn't meet your expectations. But have you ever wondered why this is happening, or if it's really a mistake? If it doesn't seem like a mistake, then perhaps it was meant to be.

This is Abraham preparing to sacrifice Isaac, this is Jacob struggling to marry Rachel. This is Joseph in prison despite his faithfulness to the Lord, this is David watching his kingdom taken by his son who coveted everything he owned, including his wives. This is you enduring your trials. But God invites you to draw near to Him, promising living water that will quench your thirst forever. It's the thirst that drives you to seek the living waters. The unreliable waters of this world compel you to search for the eternal water that will never run dry. It is the Lord Jesus Christ beckoning you through these trials to cling to the water that brings peace—a peace that cannot be given by man, for it differs from the peace the world offers.

May the Lord Jesus Christ encounter you and provide you with the water that will never run dry. For if you depart from the source of life, you will perish from thirst. Many in the world have acquired all they need, yet they still thirst for the living waters. They believed that happiness came from wealth and that wealth could purchase the happiness they sought. However, true wealth is found in the Lord Jesus Christ, for He offers a peace that no one else can. The Lord Jesus Christ bestows a peace that removes the worries of this world. Even if you clothe yourself in animal skins like John the Baptist, the joy within you will draw many to seek what you represent: and that is the Lord Jesus Christ.

# Lesson Thirty One

# LEAD OTHERS TO THE SAVIOR

The desire for large congregations may seem like a
measure of success for a church. However, many leaders
have faltered due to this very aspiration. It is important
to find contentment in what God provides.

As a preacher, persuading many to commit their lives to the Lord Jesus Christ is a significant challenge. It is a beautiful aspiration to draw crowds as seen in the Reverend Dr. Billy Graham's crusades, where hundreds would come forward to be saved. Such an ability to attract the masses is a common desire, though it often proves difficult to achieve.

No one can come to God unless God draws them. The scriptures quote the Lord Jesus Christ: "Those that You gave Me I have kept, and none of them is lost, except the son of perdition, so that the Scripture would be fulfilled." Salvation occurs at the appointed time set by God. When this time arrives for a Christian, one must be ready to guide them. The appropriate words and hymns will lead them forth.

Not all men who profess to be saved truly are. Your worth in the kingdom of God lies in that one individual you lead to the Savior. The competition to be seen as the best and to be acknowledged as the most anointed has diminished the significance of religion in many people's hearts.

Today, numerous preachers aim to gather vast audiences to capture the attention of political figures. Heads of state and nobility often visit churches with substantial memberships. Their donations, amounting to millions, please both the attendees and the clergy. Yet, such actions have greatly twisted the message of God. The chase for material riches and assets has allowed sin to permeate these places of worship. These are the desired 'men of God'—those willing to do anything to attract people to their church, while overlooking their wrongdoings. Their goal is not to honor God with large congregations, but to reap the financial benefits. True solace is found in contentment with what God has given, and therein lies true comfort. For when the Lord talks of rejoicing in heaven, it centers on the repentance of a single soul.

A reverend at an Anglican Church received a directive from her bishop to relocate and lead another diocese. She declined the transfer, citing the poverty of the church she was assigned to compared to her current station. Our devotion has shifted; Christ is no longer in our hearts. We serve the institution, not God. We serve a church that aligns with worldly desires, accepting all that sinful man wishes to preserve our wealth and possessions. You, the men of the church, have corrupted God's word, sabotaged humanity's salvation, and positioned yourselves as adversaries of God.

Rejoice in the few within your congregation, for they arrive with God's grace. The sincerity of your sermons and your defiance of earthly temptations fortify you before God. Strive to impart the truth of God and be open to welcoming them when the moment is right. Remain ever vigilant. Excel in prayer and be well-versed in hymns. Prepare hymns for the ill, for those beset by spirits, hymns that fortify the frail, and above all, seek God's fortitude in your prayers and worship.

For Worship is a powerful tool that many Christians, perhaps including yourself, have not fully appreciated. At times, a hymn can significantly impact someone's life. Often, it's not necessary to pray, but simply to lay hands on the sick and offer worship and praise, for the Lord has already provided healing. While prayer is crucial, worship can overcome many obstacles. In your gatherings for fellowship, encourage every member to sing a hymn, making it a tradition within the fellowship. That one hymn might be the key to your deliverance during a spiritual onslaught. Encourage each member to bring a song they are comfortable singing, for the Spirit of the Lord directs a person to what will dispel the darkness.

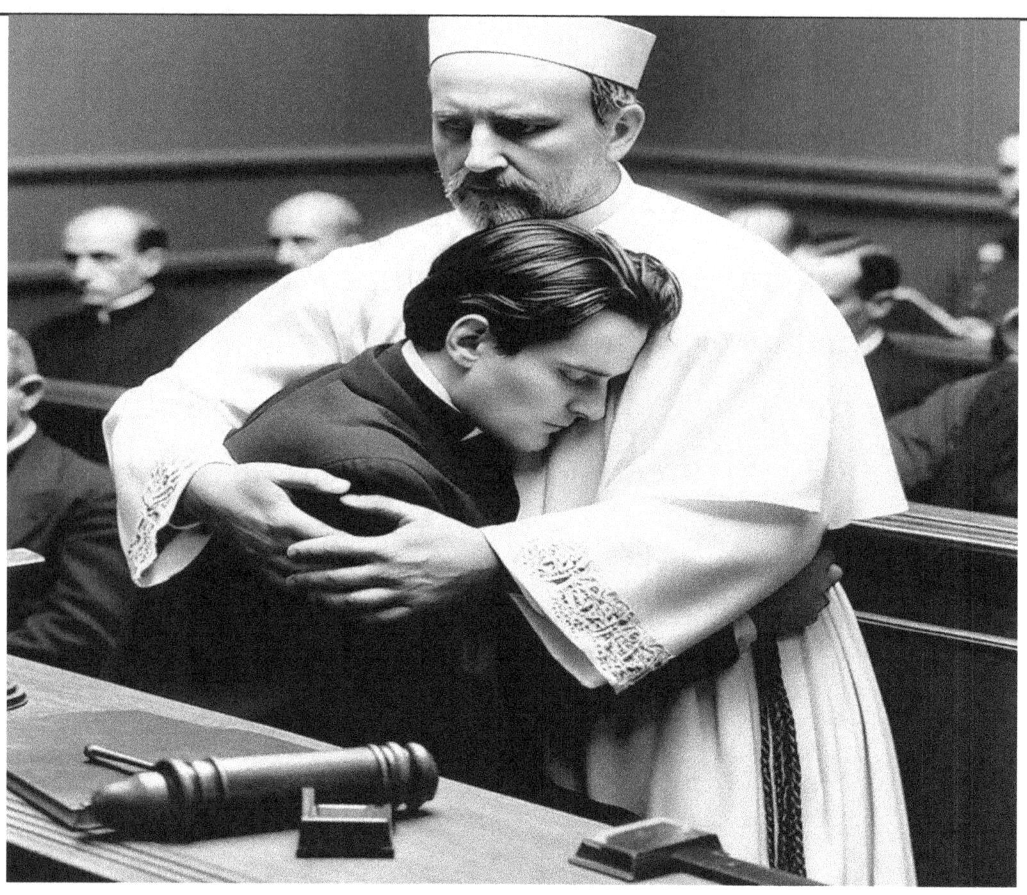

# Lesson Thirty Two

# BECOME THE SINNER

You are known for your dedication to prayer and
advocacy on behalf of others. Do you understand the
concept of intercession? To intercede means to represent
or stand in for the sinner until the sin is forgiven.

As an intercessor, it's common to forget those for whom you're interceding. You overlook the fact that you're standing in the gap. In intercession, you take on the role of the sinner before God. Invoking their names in hymns and prayers is the most effective way to advocate for them. In doing so, you embody the individual you're interceding for, standing in their stead. Nehemiah exemplifies this when he confesses, "I confess the sins we Israelites, including myself, have committed against you. We have acted very wickedly toward you. We have not obeyed the commands, decrees, and laws you gave your servant Moses." Nehemiah doesn't separate himself from Israel; he identifies with Israel's sinfulness. This marks him as a true intercessor, anointed by God.

Assume their identity, adopting their name as your own. One should never intercede for causes they do not believe in. By agreeing to intercede for another, you commit to withhold judgment. You empathize with their suffering and seek divine salvation on their behalf. The world often misunderstands the Lord's ways. It is your duty to impart that faith to others. The world remains oblivious to its sins, perceiving them as innate. However, those whom the Lord enlightens recognize and confront the world's sins, understanding the desires of their Lord.

All who believe in the Lord are called to intercede daily for the world they inhabit, which may lack faith. They are anointed to be bearers of light to the world. Instead of judging, they should teach about sin and enlighten the world about the Lord's love, aiding in its quest for the

Lord's forgiveness.

The first gift bestowed by the Lord upon all His children is the gift of intercession. You begin by interceding for yourself, seeking forgiveness for your sins. Remember also to intercede for the world you inhabit. The Holy Spirit  dwells within all who have faith in the Lord Jesus Christ. Rejoice for the sinful world you inhabit, for salvation is available to all who dwell within it. Delight in God's love, for He has granted you the key to His kingdom. This key is the Lord Jesus Christ, who selected you to represent the sinful world, to teach and disseminate His word to all who reside in this world. Rejoice for the sinners, for salvation is accessible to all who trust in the Lord Jesus Christ. Take joy in interceding for the sinful, for your own salvation was delivered through the intercession of our Lord Jesus Christ. This salvation persists through you by the might of the Holy Spirit .

# Lesson Thirty Three

## NOT ALL WRITTEN WAS INTENDED FOR TODAY

When praying and studying the Bible, it's crucial to understand that not all passages may be relevant at the current moment. There will be a time when these scriptures will become clearer and relevant.

Like many Christians, you may believe you have read and fully grasped the scriptures. You assert confidently that you have comprehended the Bible and its teachings. However, it may be disheartening to hear that there is much that remains misunderstood. Many things that the Lord Jesus Christ said appear clear, yet they are often read in the Scriptures without the intended meaning being captured. As mentioned in Daniel, some words are meant for a specific generation.

No matter how much you strive to read and comprehend these words, they may seem irrelevant to you now. Their significance will emerge in due time. When that moment arrives, you will reflect on what has been written and recognize it as the prophesied time when, according to scripture, the Lord's wrath descended upon a sinful world.

The proper interpretation of many scriptures may elude you, as their appointed time has not yet come. Consequently, their true meaning might be misunderstood.

For instance, you might often find yourself singing hymns and feel compelled to modify certain verses. This isn't to diminish their importance, but rather to strengthen the hymns in a way that supports the expansion of God's kingdom on Earth.

As culture evolves, so does the nature of worship. With the mercy and grace of God, singing these songs can lead the Holy Spirit to reveal deeper meanings, enhancing your understanding.

The disciples walked with Lord Jesus Christ, yet it is Paul's comprehension of God that laid the church's foundation. When the time was ripe, Paul arrived, reconciling the ancient teachings with the advent of Lord Jesus Christ. He elucidated the concepts of Lord Jesus Christ and the Holy Spirit, despite not being among those directly taught about the Holy Spirit by the Lord Jesus Christ. The Lord, at the appropriate time, raises individuals he has groomed for that era to clarify his word to his followers. This was apparent when Jesus spoke to the Pharisees, who did not grasp his words as they were not meant for them. However, these words resonate profoundly with many in this generation. Reading the scriptures reveals that not everything written applies to the present.

Pray to the Lord for strength and for the opening of your understanding to His written word. For those uncertain of what to say, as I write this, I hear voices in my ears, the devil loudly proclaiming his intent to kill me for my writings. To you, I am merely a man. The devil, in this mortal life, possesses all the means to combat me as a man. Yet, if we live in fear of the devil, who will fortify others to maintain their faith in Christ? I offer you strength and hope, for I understand your beliefs, and it brings me joy to see you triumph in this struggle. My prayer is for you to comprehend my words and to continue the fight. These words are meant for your understanding. The Lord has elevated me to clarify His word to His people. The time is now.

Lesson Thirty Four

# HOW TO ATTACK THE ENEMY

Being with the Lord means there is no need to fear the enemy. It's important to understand that accepting the Lord your God brings you under His protection. Stand firm in faith, and no enemy shall prevail against you.

Do not fear your enemy. If you know God, you pray and receive answers from God, there is no reason to fear your enemy. Fear is the greatest weapon used by the devil, as the devil's plans thrive on fear. Humans are consumed by fear because they understand little of the world they inhabit. They fear their identity and their future. You were born into a world rife with hate, surrounded by sin. These sins have instilled fear in your hearts.

When the devil speaks, it is with hate. When he smiles, his grin heralds death. His existence is one of sin. In our sinful lives, we seek quick fixes to feel strong. King Saul, gripped by fear, sought a witch to commune with a holy God. Similarly, we, in our fear, turn to sinners for lasting respite from our sins. Driven by fear, we embrace sin, seeking solutions within the very sin we accumulate.

Discussing fear often brings to mind the story of David and Goliath. In life, numerous fears exist. These are fears that cannot be grasped, seen, or felt with your hands, much like Goliath. Yet, they reside in your heart. The fears of poverty, disease, and death instill deep fear within man.

As a follower of the Lord Jesus Christ, He is always with you. As it was said, to the Muslim man who was once a follower of Christ, "Being saved is not merely about believing in Christ's existence. Rather, being saved brings something new within you that guides you on the right path. When you sincerely accept the Lord Jesus Christ with all your heart and soul, you allow the Holy Spirit to take control of your life."

The Lord Jesus Christ journeyed with His disciples, yet none could accompany Him to the crucifixion. Peter could not claim to know Jesus, for he did not comprehend what it meant to join Him on the cross. However, the arrival of the Holy Spirit granted power and insight. Now, humanity can grasp and possess the bravery to advocate for the kingdom of heaven's welfare. The Holy Spirit 's advent simplified the disciples' comprehension of God. Through this understanding, the disciples were willing to lay down their lives for the teachings of the Lord Jesus Christ. For the Holy Spirit , upon arriving, enlightens humanity that this world holds value for those who fail to perceive and acknowledge the benevolence of Jesus Christ and the heavenly realm where He rules.

For this reason, being in Christ likens you to David. He may not have had the stature of Samson, but that was of little consequence. To the enemy, David  appeared small and insignificant, a diminutive figure armed only with sticks and stones. Yet, within David's heart lay the resolve to confront Goliath on that fateful day. The Holy Spirit  endows you with the courage and fortitude to confront your fears. David understood that what resided within him surpassed anything the world could perceive. What lies within you is greater than what is visible to the world.

The purpose of preaching the gospel is to reveal to the world the God it has overlooked. The goal is not merely to assemble congregations, but to fulfill the Lord's will. For God's joy differs from human reasoning. Through your words, you impart the Lord's message into the hearts of men. These individuals navigate the world fearlessly. The Lord seeks such men who can steadfastly confront and denounce sin. They are similar to John the Baptist, who dares to challenge kings and call for their repentance. These are the men upon whom the Holy Spirit confers His name with pride. They represent heaven and wield the power of the Father.

# Lesson Thirty Five

## ASK FOR SIGNS

**When you pray, do you look for signs from God? People who sincerely ask for signs from Him tend to notice and understand these divine messages.**

The heart harbors desires, yet these desires cannot be fulfilled simultaneously. Such desires often become vulnerabilities. It is upon these weaknesses that satan preys, causing suffering. For some, it may manifest as fear, theft, adultery, or alcoholism. These frailties are the footholds the devil uses to thwart the children of God. You may achieve much, but a single frailty can consistently hold you back. Many yearn for marriage, which God cherishes, extolling its virtues when a man finds a woman. However, the critical question remains: is the person you are with the one God intended for you? Discerning signs to confirm if your blessings are from God is essential. Struggles may arise in life because what you possess was not given by God. Jobs acquired through bribery, influence built on falsehoods—these are the origins you forget as you seek the Lord's intervention to amend the chaos you've wrought. It is crucial to seek signs and let God be part of all new beginnings.

During marriage counseling, it was noted that some attendees were physically present but mentally elsewhere, questioning their reasons for marriage. It's observed that individuals sometimes marry for misguided reasons such as wealth, family pressure, or even through the influence of witchcraft, which is considered a means to compel someone into marriage. This practice isn't limited to women; men also partake. Despite societal shifts labeling witchcraft as archaic, it persists. Consequently, marriages founded on such grounds rather than love or divine blessing often lead to sorrow.

It's important to encourage children to pray for their future spouses from an early age. One should seek divine guidance to discern if their current partner is truly the right one for them. This applies not just to singles, but also to those who are married.

God Provides Three Signs. The journey of Lord Jesus Christ is encapsulated in three signs: His birth as a man, His death as a man, and His resurrection as God. He declared, "I can destroy this temple and rebuild it in three days," signifying the three days from His death to resurrection. He offers three signs in response to your prayers. No matter how many signs the devil may present, he cannot provide all three signs before God.

When seeking divine guidance, it is suggested to request three signs from God. If you find yourself admired by multiple suitors and are uncertain of whom God has chosen for you, seek a sign. Just as Sarah was cherished by God and irreplaceable in Abraham's household, you may ask for a specific sign: let the man who is to be my husband present me with a shilling coin. Upon the fulfillment of one sign, proceed to request the next, and then the third. Be mindful that God communicates in various forms, and remain receptive to His signs.

You may request a coin, anticipating its physical manifestation, yet God may unveil it within a dream. It is in these moments that Christians ought to pay close attention to their dreams. God communicates through dreams just as He provides tangible signs. He conversed with Solomon in a dream, bestowing upon him the immense gift of wisdom. God's voice resonates in dreams, and many scriptures were revealed in such visions. He speaks daily. God will communicate and reveal the signs of your quest.

# Lesson Thirty Six

# GOD SEPARATED
# THE LIGHT FROM THE DARKNESS

**The coming of the Lord Jesus Christ was predestined well before the creation of humankind. With his divine foresight, God recognized the plight of the fallen angels and foresaw their impact on humanity.**

The general depiction of satan from the beginning portrays him as a serpent in Genesis. This imagery is the most vivid representation of the devil in the early texts. A thorough reading of Genesis reveals an understanding that the mission of the Lord Jesus Christ on Earth was predetermined long before the creation of the world.

Before the creation of man, God was aware of the fallen angels and their potential influence on humanity, necessitating a savior. Everything that transpired in the Garden was foreknown by the Lord; nothing occurred without His knowledge. The presence of the devil in the Garden reveals the truth of God's plan for mankind—a plan that unfolded entirely within that setting. The Lord was cognizant of the devil's limitations and knew that satan could never contend with His character.

As previously documented, I reiterate to everyone. Your journey on this earth is influenced by the company you keep. The nature of your actions, whether good or bad, is determined by who accompanies you. The Lord Jesus Christ taught that it's not about what enters but rather what exits. To clarify, it is the one residing in your heart that dictates your words and deeds. If it is satan, your actions and speech will reflect his presence. Conversely, if it is the Lord Jesus Christ, your fruits will be the measure by which you are judged.

In my writings, I have noted that the crucifixion of Jesus Christ was influenced by satan. It is evident when one observes how people behaved around the Lord Jesus Christ; these influences become apparent.

The Holy Spirit  enlightens individuals about the nature of the devil. satan is considered the most malevolent entity one could encounter. Upon learning of his words and actions, one may question how anyone could profess worship to such a being. It's crucial to understand the gravity of whom you speak.

satan is often depicted as a being without hope, similar to a prisoner awaiting execution. His smile is typically linked with malevolence. Man cannot coexist with satan, in life or in death. He harbors animosity towards God and humanity because humans are God's image. After wasting his existence with God, he now aims to ruin God's creations.

The devil utters no praise for God. His tongue never weaves words of admiration for the divine. In his speech, there is no encouragement, only the specter of demise. He lauds the sinners and those who tread the path of vice, naming them his progeny. The devil is well-versed in every profane song that the market bears, familiar with the latest dances and each unholy tune that resounds. His mastery of their rhythms is evident. Through his songs and dances, one can discern the mark he has left on the entertainment industry.

He utters the most vulgar words one could hear. He persistently insults God and His devotees. He mocks the celestial angels as fools for not partaking in his rebellion. He boasts of being superior to God and speaks ill of the divine teachings. In doing so, he deceives the faithful into thinking he is a deity. satan operates in shadows, inflicting harm upon humanity who remains oblivious to his presence.

"In the beginning, there was light," and God saw that the light was good, so He separated the light from the darkness. From Genesis, we witness the emergence of humanity from darkness. The Lord Jesus Christ entered the world and became the light. As stated in the Gospel of John, "In Him was life, and that life was the light of all mankind. The light shines in the darkness, and the darkness has not overcome it."

Jesus is the light, the force that divided the world from darkness from the outset, as chronicled in Genesis. This light continues to shine, as depicted in the Gospel of John, and the darkness shall not overcome it, as proclaimed in Revelation.

# Lesson Thirty Seven

## THE LORD JESUS CHRIST WAS ENVIED

satan will cause those around you to despise you. The only
method satan uses to combat God is through Man. You
will be subjected to envy just as the Lord Jesus Christ
was. For you are beloved by God, and satan is aware that
what he inflicts upon humanity,
he also does to God.

We acknowledge a sovereign king who descended from the heavens for the betterment of humanity. This majestic being is the Lord Jesus Christ, not just a mortal but God in human form. It is indeed profound to reflect on the extent of God's love, evidenced by the supreme sacrifice for the sake of humankind. The baffling question remains: despite beholding the Lord's splendor, why does satan relentlessly continue to betray Him? Such conduct may be ascribed to Envy, where a being, after observing the divine radiance, opts to disgrace his Maker.

Envy is a malady, one that all humanity should combat. This affliction has permeated the daily lives of people. As scripture has recorded, the Lord our God was envied by the Pharisees. They each admired His authority, His deeds, and His teaching style. Yet, none were willing to request, "Lord, teach us." Envy can take root in a person, with satan sowing its seeds. Just as the Lord our God faced envy, so does man. The devil seeks to turn those around you into adversaries, well aware that he cannot contend with your God. He knows he cannot wage and win a war against your God. satan is aware that you are chosen by God, and when he assails you, he is challenging God Himself. However, the Holy Spirit reassures you; with my mercy upon you, anyone who assails you assails me. Henceforth, all your conflicts become the Lord's. This promise was also made to Abraham: "I will bless those who bless you, and whoever curses you, I will curse." And to the world, He declared: "Whoever listens to you listens to me. Whoever rejects you rejects me. And whoever rejects me rejects the one who sent me."

When such promises are made, God does not whisper in secrecy; He proclaims them so loudly that even the devil can hear and comprehend. If the devil assails you, it is as if he has assailed God Himself, for your actions are not your own but for God. Thus, the devil is defeated in both spirit and flesh. As you are safeguarded, satan seeks methods to afflict you. His sole avenue is to stir up adversaries to do his bidding.

The Pharisees, out of envy for the Lord Jesus Christ, opened their hearts to evil and opposed their own God. Who among you would be content after death to discover that you had opposed God? Many, my friends, have unwittingly opposed God Himself. Others who have opposed you have, in fact, opposed God. This is why the Lord Jesus Christ taught us to love our enemies. Without love, how can we reveal the truth to them?

Jesus entered a world that had unwittingly turned against Him. He sacrificed His life for you, despite knowing you might not care for Him. Yet, through His death, the truth was revealed: about an adversary who roams to dismantle what God has created. This foe, satan, tirelessly strives to undermine all that represents God.

Stand firm in the love of our Father. Be bold in the face of the world's hate. Understand that it is not you who is hated, but the Lord God whom you serve. Remember, it is not the people you walk with who despise you, but satan who has taken root in the hearts of your adversaries. Through them, the fruits of satan become apparent. Comprehending these words, you will learn to forgive, to be patient, and to walk among your enemies, displaying the love, joy, and mercy that the Lord God has bestowed upon you.

My friends and children of God, it is a privilege that the Lord God cherishes you, choosing you to be part of His kingdom. The scriptures abound with tales of satan and the formidable strength of these spirits over mankind. Yet, therein lies your human strength. To please God, you need not construct a synagogue as Solomon did, nor offer a thousand sheep as David did. You simply need to demonstrate your love for Him, worshipping only Him and no other God. Through the love of God in the Lord Jesus Christ, all sins were cleansed, making humanity a treasured possession of the Father. This love is personified in the Lord Jesus Christ himself, and by believing in this love and adhering to His commands, you embody that love in the Father.

God created you for the purpose of worshiping Him. However, you have chosen to worship satan and have forgotten the Lord your God. You should employ love to conquer your enemies. Allow this love to draw them to our Father. The Lord our God is constantly at work, transforming lives, and in time, your enemies may become a pillar of His Gospel.

# Lesson Thirty Eight

## YOU HAVE A GOD WHO LOVES YOU

You possess a God whose essence is love. You ought to appear as though you are cherished. You hold the wealth the world requires, yet seem uncherished. Accept God's love and live as a genuine reflection of God's image.

You are loved by a God whose love is far greater than you could ever conceive. The depth of this love is beyond imagination, so profound that He would willingly sacrifice Himself for your sins so you may enter heaven. The world may despise you and continue to do so, failing to comprehend your devotion to your God. Your purpose in this life is to disseminate this love to the world, to help many understand His enduring love that has existed since the beginning.

You speak of love, yet you appear unloved. You ought to embody the love that the world requires. You ought to forgive those who wrong you. You ought to discern the truth. You ought to courageously proclaim to the world your God's perspective on their wrongdoings. For God says;

"They make decisions without considering me, their God, and instead follow the world's reasoning. Such decisions have caused suffering among the poor and left widows weeping in despair due to injustice. The judges now favor the wealthy, seizing and claiming land under the guise of leadership."

Church leaders have become powerless and have committed many wrongs. They have aligned themselves with wrongdoing to the extent that the world doubts God's presence among them. They may dress like my followers, but I am not within them. They are honored by the wealthy and the wicked. These leaders welcome them to lavish feasts and seat them in places of honor. They praise the wrongdoers and neglect to admonish them for their sins.

They no longer represent me. The world mocks me, the Lord their God, who is said to work through them. The world scoffs at my word, which was written to unite it. They say your word is outdated, that it belongs to the past. Our world today is advanced. Look at our achievements. Observe the height of our buildings. Your word is deemed insufficient to unite the world now. My people have turned against me, aligning with wealth and opting for worldly pleasures.

My people are engulfed in sin, and there seems to be no one to deliver my message to them. They continue in their sinful ways, yet you remain seated among them in those churches. You sit amidst my people, reading my words, yet not from your heart. You proclaim my words to the world as if you stand with me, yet you are not by my side. You have not followed my rules and commands, and as a result, my sheep have gone astray. You have twisted my word to the word that favours sin. You have brought evil into my house, and you call my name together with evil.

The Lord God, your God, is a God of truth and holds love for the truth. He fashioned this world with love and for the sake of truth. He perceives through darkness and into the depths of a man's heart. He observes all that is beyond human sight. He looks further than what the world can perceive. The world is my beloved, and you are my visage upon this earth. You embody ME, the truth. I am your God, the truth of the world. Yet, you have allied with evil to expunge truth from the world. And you surmise that I, the Lord your God, will observe from the heavens and let this transpire.

I came into this world to reveal the truth. Yet, you opt to hide my truth behind my very name. You charm me with songs of happiness that do not please me, for your hearts are far away. Your prayers do not reach me anymore, for I am not within you. And still, the world sees you as possessing me. They consider you to be with me at all times. And yet, you avoid even speaking my name.

Your responsibilities have shifted from serving your God to earning a livelihood. You no longer act for my benefit but for your own. You aspire to worldly positions, competing for roles in my church as secular individuals do. You resort to worldly  judges for dispute resolution without seeking guidance from me, your God, yet you claim to represent me?

# Lesson Thirty Nine

## GOD HAS HIS TIME

Transformation is a journey marked by both progress and setbacks. It is essential to exercise patience and understanding towards individuals within the Christian community who are undergoing personal growth. It is worth noting that God operates within His own time-line, which may not align with human expectations.

The transformative journey is one of comprehending the Lord's ways. This path is as intricate as the ways of God. As previously stated, the Lord instructs you in His ways before sending you forth. It is through you that others come to know His true nature. Grasping the ways of God is so challenging that even the devil has not succeeded in mastering them.

Many have undergone transformation to grasp the ways of the Lord. Yet, they often conclude, "One cannot fully comprehend God's ways. His ways are distinct from human understanding. Our thinking is too rudimentary and constrained, leading us to lament even when the struggle is nearly finished."

Becoming a believer in Christ brings one into pure communion with the Holy Spirit. From that moment, there is a belief that God will manage all things. This was evident among the disciples and those who recognized Jesus as the promised Messiah. They believed their struggles with Rome had ended. However, the Lord's journey and battles were vastly different from what Israel had anticipated.

Receiving a message from the Lord about marriage often leads one to expect the event to occur within a day or two. This misconception is why many lose faith. The spiritual battle is waged between good and evil. Its intensity stems from being born into sin and enslaved by it. The scriptures say: your ancestors sinned and have passed away, yet their sins linger with you. The devil holds you prisoner to generational curses that are largely unknown to you.

An American once inquired, "Why do Black Americans hold us accountable for enslavement? It happened 200 years ago, and I wasn't even alive." If I had the chance to respond, I would tell him, "The legacy of your ancestors doesn't cease with their passing; it persists through generations, just as their blessings do."

It is distinct for Cain was to be condemned to hell for murdering Abel, and Cain's descendants suffering on earth for Abel's blood. David's sin of adultery had repercussions through his sons, who dishonored his wives and their sister. Although David repented and was forgiven by God, it is not clear if he repented for his sons and grandsons. The scriptures illustrate how Job continually interceded for his children. Similarly, Abraham's blessings were inherited by Isaac, Jacob, and eventually reached the Lord Jesus Christ. Sin necessitates an intercessor. When seeking God's intervention, understanding the reason for any delay is crucial, for God designed a world where struggle is unnecessary.

Many do not question God about the reasons for their inability to have children. When the disciples asked Jesus whose sin caused a man's blindness, He replied that it was neither of his parents'. It is important to seek understanding from God. While seeking immediate healing, one must consider the generational sins of their ancestors which may not have been repented for. The scriptures recount how satan laid claim to Moses. Many accept the scriptural account of Moses' holy death. Yet, it was the archangel Michael who countered satan, declaring, "The Lord rebuke you."

The devil persistently tempts you to join him in sin, representing a spiritual battle that led Jesus Christ to sacrifice Himself for humanity's sins—a sacrifice so profound that even Sodom and Gomorrah might have been spared. Jesus became the mediator between God and man, ending the reign of sin. Thus, the Lord wages His battles in a unique way.

You may not realize the sacrifices made by your ancestors who dedicated themselves, including you, to satan. Your forefathers offered sacrifices and handed you over to the devil. Spiritual spouses are believed to hinder you from marrying anyone as they claim ownership. The pursuit of wealth has led people to align their descendants with satan.

The Lord has His own methods of resolving conflicts, and this does not occur in mere minutes or hours, but rather in His divine timing. If you pray and dedicate yourselves properly to the Lord, He will indeed address your suffering. However, no one can act rightly before God unless God Himself permits it. He has an appointed time for each person, and it is important to recognize that you should not just wait, but actively engage in God's predetermined plan for your aspirations. The scriptures illustrate that Jesus was not apprehended sooner because His time had not yet arrived; God has a designated time for all things.

## Lesson Forty

# THE POWER IS IN
# THE NAME OF JESUS

The name of Jesus was bestowed upon all humanity as a means
to combat darkness. No hymn, worship song, or prayer is
complete without using the name of Jesus Christ.
It is in the name of Jesus that power resides,
and it is this power that removes obstacles.

The gospel you preach has weakened the path to salvation, for the name of the Lord Jesus Christ has been forgotten. In your battles with the devil, the significance of Jesus' name should be evident. Consider the unsaved; how will they come to value the name of the Lord Jesus Christ?

Songs are often sung differently by non-Christians simply because they omit Christ's name, transforming these hymns into secular tunes for any occasion. Your walk with God didn't begin on the day of your salvation; it commenced at birth. The Lord has meticulously prepared your path towards the day of your encounter with Him. Despite varied backgrounds, many of which scarcely align with devout living, you outwardly display Christian ways, yet God does not dwell in your hearts. Christianity and Christ have become mere labels. There is pride in the Christian identity, but not necessarily in Jesus Christ. This is similar to the pride some feel in being American or British, based on perceived superiority over others. Leading a heart to God is beyond human capability; it is God alone who understands what brings joy or sorrow to man, and He alone knows when one might yield.

Many church members worship the Lord yet remain unsaved. Some attend church for fellowship, others for lack of anywhere else to go, and some for the love of the choir. Their presence in church is positive, but God seeks a personal encounter with them in His timing. No matter the eloquence of the preaching, it is not enough to convert them. As the scriptures state, 'No one can come to me unless the Father who sent me draws him.' This underscores the importance of sincere worship. We must not stifle the name of Jesus but ensure it is proclaimed in our sermons and songs for all to hear.

A preacher delivered a sermon that lasted over 30 minutes until the service concluded. Throughout his discourse, the name Jesus Christ was never mentioned. The closest reference made was to 'the Lord,' and even this was rare. This omission raises questions about the nature of the gospel being preached to the congregation. Without mentioning His name, how will they understand the power it holds? Such avoidance allows the world to pass judgment on you and the God you worship, perceiving Him as inactive or nonexistent. It suggests a failure to adhere to His directives. Recall His words to the disciples, "How long shall I stay with you? How long shall I put up with you?"

You have strayed from the Lord's ministry on this earth, and it is time to awaken. Your gospel preaches prosperity, which is evident among you, the preachers of the word. Your gospel has shifted from the Lord's words in the scriptures to the world's miserable life. People are drawn to your gospel because you speak of the injustices, poverty, and diseases in their lives, yet you overlook their permanence. Poverty and disease will persist, but the true joy for a man in suffering is found in the Lord Jesus Christ. The Lord is omnipresent, omniscient, and provides for everyone in their actions and being. Your duty is to help mankind recognize that the Lord is with them at all times. Not everyone will overcome disease or acquire the wealth you proclaim from the pulpit. However, every person can find joy in the Lord Jesus Christ, for He grants the fullness of His spirit to man, and that fullness is the capacity to find happiness, even amidst poverty.

# Lesson Forty One

# EMBRACE YOUR SUFFERING

The Lord God understands all forms of suffering. Some may think that God is unaware of their pain, but the truth is your faith endures because of God's presence. Embrace your suffering, knowing that God is by your side throughout this trial.

Always remember, the Lord is your shepherd; He has fought all your battles. Whenever you call on His mercy, He draws nearer to you.

May these words bring hope and strength to all who are in sorrow. Let them be a source of courage to maintain your faith during challenging times. Many will read these words and find themselves filled with questions. You may wonder why you've faced trials, including stays in a mental hospital, or why you were tempted without a clear path to escape. Especially when you felt close to the Lord, worshipping Him daily, praying multiple times a day, and constantly leading in praise and worship.

## LISTEN TO WHAT THE LORD DECLARES;

*"You had to endure what you did to become what I envisioned for you. Jesus had to suffer on the cross to attain glory among his followers. Peter had to deny me thrice and acknowledge his frailty before I proclaimed him the cornerstone of my church. David had to confront Goliath to prove to the world his divine favor. Jacob labored for fourteen years to marry Rachel. Abraham was willing to sacrifice Isaac to demonstrate his faith in me."*

*"Even though I knew the hearts of all my servants, they had to undergo these trials so that my name would be exalted. I select those whom I love and wish to serve me; they do not choose me. I have my methods of preparing them for their tasks on this earth. Everything you have endured*

*was orchestrated by me, for it is the purpose for which I created you to fulfill on this earth."*

Many expect a seamless existence as God's anointed, believing they should be powerful enough to conquer all challenges. But, are they mightier than God Himself, who faced humiliation by His creation, the devil? The devil, who tempted Him with kingdoms in exchange for worship? Who decrees that being chosen by God shields one from disgrace? Every stalwart figure in the scriptures endured humiliation while walking with the Lord. The apostles were persecuted, Jeremiah was branded a liar, Jezebel threatened Elijah's life causing him to flee, and Moses feared returning to Egypt after slaying an Egyptian. I, too, was labeled insane and disbelieved, finding myself isolated in a mental institution, confronting the devil alone.

Today, you embody the roles of Moses, Elijah, and the Apostles as depicted in the scriptures, though they have long departed. You are the beacon of God's kingdom, destined to endure challenges similar to the trials faced by Jesus Christ. Persevere, for ultimately, you shall be uplifted, and His name shall be glorified by the world. Stand firm in your faith.

# Lesson Forty Two

## GOD HAS HIS WAYS

God has various methods of nurturing those He has chosen. What may seem like suffering is actually the path that shapes you into what the Lord intends for you.

Many misunderstand the ways of God, thinking that minor setbacks are signs of His failure. Often, these are preparations for greater things. As King David said, "Weeping may stay for the night, but rejoicing comes in the morning."

But If weeping may endure for the night and joy comes in the morning, then one must seek Him in the night to behold His glory in the morning.

A man had been unemployed for three years when the Lord vowed to provide for him. Through his mother, a widow, God intended to care for him. He experienced the same anguish as Elijah when he realized it was the widow who would feed him—a widow with a son and no food. Yet, Elijah was never alone; he was with the Lord God who knew his journey. This widow was destined to do something for Elijah that would not only fortify him but also all future generations who would learn of Elijah. You may feel like a failure because your life's events differ from your expectations. The Lord is unique and often uses challenging experiences to help you see and understand Him. The man's mother invited him to fellowship, not realizing it was the Lord calling him. His time had arrived to leave worldly pursuits and embrace his true purpose. During those days, the Lord remained silent about him among the praying brethren. He sat among fellow worshippers who possessed spiritual gifts, yet he had none. In his heart, he yearned not for gifts but for employment to restore the life he once knew. He would confess inwardly, "I am not here to serve God; I am here to find a job, and that's why I pray."

Peter was unaware that the Lord had selected  him to advance His mission. Unlike the two disciples who debated who was the greatest in heaven, Peter did not engage in such disputes. Throughout the scriptures, Peter is depicted as a man who remained with Jesus out of love for Him. He expressed a willingness to die alongside Jesus, but Jesus knew that Peter could not bear that burden. Peter did not seek status; he recognized  Jesus as Lord and cherished being in  His presence. Peter humbly acknowledged his unique place among the disciples and in God's heart. God shielded Peter from harm, yet the spiritual world was aware of him. satan, recognizing Peter's favor with the Lord, sought permission to tempt him, aiming to challenge his devotion. The intent behind Peter's trials was not to sever his bond with the Lord but to assess his fidelity. Despite denying Jesus thrice, Peter returned to the Lord. In contrast, Judas, who also denied the Lord, took his own life, for such love was absent in his heart.

There is an aspect of Peter's faith in Jesus Christ that transcends verbal explanation. The love one holds for the Lord is beyond the realm of words. When you draw the Lord near and surrender yourself entirely, He indeed assumes control over everything you possess. It reflects in your speech, your worship, and your prayers. Jesus questioned Peter three times about his love for Him. From that moment, Christ dwelled within Peter, guiding him until the conclusion of his earthly journey. The Lord embodies you, and every word you utter is His proclamation.

# Lesson Forty Three

## THE LORD IS WITH YOU

You may shed tears believing you have failed, but it's a misunderstanding of your setbacks. When God opens the doors to greatness, there is often a failure at the beginning to help you recognize the path to that greatness.

When you walk with the Lord, He guides you. His guidance is unlike any man's; He operates through you. His protection is manifested in the words He instills in you. The tears you've shed over perceived failures were never truly failures, but rather God's unique methods. "Tears may come in the night" speaks to those who have faith in the Lord Jesus Christ. You weep, not realizing the battle is nearly victorious.

A man wept when he could not win the heart of the woman he loved, named Betty. He believed she was the one he was destined to marry.

*THIS ORDEAL CAN SERVE AS A LESSON ABOUT DIVINE INTENTIONS AND THE MALEVOLENT WAYS IN WHICH EVIL CAN BE INSTIGATED AROUND MAN.*

Every man in this man's circle began to fall for Betty. She layed with each of them, except for the man who had envisioned marrying her. She chose the company of men who offered her no promises over the one who offered her marriage.

*THIS STRUGGLE DEMONSTRATES HOW ADVERSITY CAN CHALLENGE ONE'S FAITH.*

In the end, Betty did not marry any of these men. When the man she left found another woman and married, the others abandoned Betty, leaving her unmarried.

*THE LESSON*

The devil operates by exploiting evil hearts to perpetrate wickedness. After using them, he abandons them to their ruined lives. He incites them to kill and mocks their own demise. He corrupts the sanctity of relationships and revels in the resulting afflictions. He takes pleasure in humanity's defiance of God. His battle against God is waged through humans. Be vigilant and observe the world around you. Recognize the extent of evil that pervades, child of God. But always bear in mind, the Lord is with you, and no malevolence shall prevail.

# Lesson Forty Four

## THE LORD SPEAKS

The Lord communicates, and when He does, His voice
is loud enough for you to hear. Yet, despite the clarity,
many have struggled to comprehend His ways of
communication.

As you journey through life, your perceptions will differ from those of others. This doesn't mean something is amiss; it simply means you are unique. When I say the Lord speaks, some will concur, while others will not. What escapes many is that we are all measured differently by God, particularly regarding our purpose on this earth. Consider Peter and Judas Iscariot. In the eyes of Lord Jesus Christ, they stood on different grounds. He was aware of their identities and destinies, yet they did not. As Jesus advanced in His mission, He often mentioned Judas and Peter in His stories. However, they were never granted the insight into His words about them. To Peter, He said, "From now on, you will be a fisher of men." And He declared, "I chose the twelve of you myself, yet one among you is a devil."

The Lord Jesus Christ spoke, yet neither of the two understood His words. Similarly, the Lord speaks to you daily. He calls out to you every moment, but you fail to hear. You endure suffering in this world under dark influences, yet you shut your eyes to the light. Given that the light has come into the world, no one should claim they do not see it. For the light is not hidden under a bed but is hung openly for all to see.

In the eyes of God, you are all unique. God has summoned you for a singular purpose, yet by diverse routes. You possess varied gifts, tailored to your designated role in service to the Lord on this earth. The Lord is aware of your destination, even if you are not fully acquainted with the path. The timing of the Lord's return is uncertain to you, but it is known to the Father. If you believe that the world is beyond God's influence, you are deceiving yourselves.

When Elijah appealed to the Lord, he mentioned the 7000. Who are these seven thousand? They are not a reserve force for a final battle. Instead, they are individuals unknown to the world, who are themselves unaware of their significant role in God's kingdom. At the appointed time, the Lord summons them to fulfill His work. John the Baptist was one of the 7000. His purpose was to declare the advent of the Lord's time. Once he completed this mission, his role was fulfilled. He resided in the wilderness, unspoken of until he began his public ministry. There, in solitude, he communed with God, who readied him for the moment of his divine calling.

There are 7,000 who have walked with God and understand His ways. These are the men of God through whom He speaks to the world. He has preserved them for the time when He needs them. Who among you knew of the 12 disciples? Where did they come from? Before Jesus, they were not devoted servants of God. One was a tax collector, and another a fisherman. Yet, God knew them, and when the time came, they abandoned everything to follow Him. Among them were those who recognized the Lord but were not committed to Him. Therefore, I tell you, love all men, whether they are in sin or not. There are many great men of God who have not yet seen the light, but their time is approaching. They traverse the most sinful parts of the world. However, the Lord recognizes them and when He gazes upon them, He declares,

'That boy is David, My king of Israel.'

Let's shift our perspective on sinners. It is through them that we discovered a committed spiritual warrior who penned profound words—Paul. We should remain attentive to the Lord's voice. Our struggle should be to listen to the Lord, for once He begins to speak, the noise of the world fades away.

# Lesson Forty Five

# UNDER SPIRITUAL ATTACK

Frequently, spiritual attacks take on physical forms that are visible to the naked eye. Identifying these signs is essential for recognizing when one is undergoing a spiritual attack.

Spiritual battles manifest physically, yet only a handful of the living are aware of them. As one contends with life's struggles, numerous spiritual signs appear in our world. However, only a select few are knowledgeable and able to comprehend these signs.

Such signs may originate from your dreams, your surroundings, and your physical sensations. You might not speak much about the world around you, yet these signs are evident in your gaze. Encountering uncommon snakes, insects, rats, frogs, snails, and other creatures in your home can signify that you are experiencing a spiritual attack, a physical manifestation of the spiritual world.

The same struggles persist as we engage in prayer and worship. satan continues to battle against our efforts to pray and worship. This is why I emphasized the importance of prayer before any service in my previous writing. If you find yourself stuck, repeating the same words during prayer, or if you forget the lyrics of a hymn and have to start over, these may be indications of a spiritual battle. It is at these moments that many feel compelled to abandon their prayers and worship. They might later say with a sense of pride, "Whenever I begin to pray, sleep overcomes me, and I cannot complete my prayer." Yet, curiously, these same individuals can perform other activities without succumbing to sleep.

These are the physical signs of satan's resistance to your prayers. You undergo these experiences, yet your minds are not open to recognizing the battles you face. You wander through this world questioning the existence of the Lord. Why do you struggle to pray and worship? Why is it easier to adore all songs except the one that deeply resonates with your pains?

satan battles, and the Lord permits this to enlighten you about the adversary. King David was with Saul for years, yet the Lord never allowed David to harm Saul. Although David recognized the enemy and understood his methods, he could not harm Saul because it was the Lord who fought his battles, not David himself. Eventually, David overcame the enemy peacefully. God desires for you to recognize satan and the ways he has led mankind astray. He wants you to comprehend all satanic methods, after which you will grasp the ways of God. satan strives to prevent you from praying and worshipping, as these are the tools the Lord has bestowed upon humanity. He weakens your resolve in God's word and extinguishes your desire to worship, thus ensuring your bondage to sin.

I tell you this: when you begin to pray and notice you're stuck on the same prayer, proceed to another section. If you're giving thanks and can't finish, shift to seeking forgiveness. If you're reciting the Lord's Prayer and can't continue, choose a worship song instead. Return to the prayer after the hindrance is lifted. Similarly, if your voice wanes during a song, keep singing until the end. An evil spirit may be interfering, but don't cease worship due to an imperfect tone. Continue; your worship is for healing from God, not for the world's approval. God cherishes persistence, which demonstrates your love  and belief in salvation through Him alone. Persistent worship wins spiritual battles, and within each song there is a prayer, persistence forces the devil to release you.

Lesson Forty Six

# SEEK FOR THE MERCY OF GOD

What maintains humility in this world? It is the ability to walk humbly in poverty and remain humble amidst great wealth. What preserved King David's humility during his reign and led to Saul's downfall? It is known as the mercy of God.

The mercy of God is beyond human explanation, yet it is experienced uniquely by many. It is a paramount defining factor in how one lives and follows His path in this world. Consider the stories of those who were humble and then changed upon attaining a certain status. Recall King Saul, who began his reign with humility but later changed, losing that humility.

I can recount tales of numerous global leaders who started humbly but were transformed by power. How many of you started with nothing and now fear mingling with the less fortunate? There was a female donor from England, originally from Uganda. Her journey took her from Uganda to study in Denmark and then to England, where she met a wealthy Englishman who provided her with an affluent life. Having become wealthy, she now scrutinizes her surroundings for cleanliness to prevent illness.

What maintains a man's humility? What sustains his character, even as he gains greater respect in life? How did David remain humble, continuing to honor the prophets after ascending to the throne? What drove the disciples, Paul, and others depicted in the scriptures to persevere, fully aware of their imminent fate? We attribute this to the mercy of God. It is not merely the capacity to endure but the grace received through faith in the Lord.

Drawing the Lord near makes Him a part of you. This aligns with the scripture, "If He is within me, who can be against me?" It is His mercy that places His name on your lips in times of poverty and fortifies it when you are affluent. God's mercy reflects His character in dealing with humanity. It is God's culture, as portrayed by man in this world, that allows everyone to recognize His blessings. This grace is not for all, but for those who have faith in Him. To these faithful, He draws near, teaching them His ways, helping them to discern Him from evil, and enabling them to testify to His glory with honesty and courage. They are His children, and He remains with them until the end. Seek God's mercy daily, and let Him steer you to the very end.

# Lesson Forty Seven

## SEEK THE HOLY SPIRIT

Do not take offense at the pursuit of the Holy Spirit . The
Holy Spirit  is God Himself. Across all scriptures, the
Holy Spirit  represents the beginning. In seeking Him,
you will witness the marvels of God's power.

Who can elucidate the Holy Spirit and its workings? The Spirit of God has been acknowledged from the dawn of creation to the final verse of the scriptures. Despite extensive writings, humanity has struggled to comprehend its true essence. Through the Holy Spirit, the Virgin Mary conceived a child. The same Spirit led the Lord Jesus Christ into the wilderness. Although Jesus Christ was weak, the Spirit of the Lord fortified Him. True worship includes acknowledging the power of the Holy Spirit .

The goodness of the Holy Spirit is beyond imagination. By the power of the Holy Spirit, Mary conceived a child without knowing a man. This child is Lord Jesus Christ, who sacrificed His blood for your sins.

Appreciating the works of the Holy Spirit is not offensive. The scriptures distinctly mention the works of the Holy Spirit during Jesus's time on earth. They also clearly convey the Lord's words as He was concluding His earthly journey. Just as the Holy Spirit accompanied the Lord Jesus Christ on earth, He is with us today. Although the Lord Jesus Christ ascended to heaven in physical form, the Holy Spirit represents Jesus Himself.

The Holy Spirit is present on Earth to assist you in your difficulties. If you seek Him, He will respond, for He is God Himself, the Father and the Son.

# Lesson Forty Eight

# WAITING UPON THE LORD

**The pain of awaiting the Lord's timing is unmatched. Not knowing the moment or the day requires you to be strengthened to endure. For As you wait, the success of others in darkness, whose hearts are not with God, seem to achieve great success, challenging your faith in the Lord.**

In times when life appears to be faltering, maintaining belief is crucial. The most significant challenge often resides in patiently waiting upon the Lord. Not all have the grace to wait with patience, and many stumble along this path. It is a widespread belief that prayers will be answered quickly, perhaps today or tomorrow.

Only a handful of individuals have the grace to peer into the spiritual realm. However, there is more to it than what is immediately apparent. Numerous people have seen their future through revelations in the spiritual world and are still waiting for its realization. Then, what about those who neither dream nor receive messages from God? They need the strength and vitality that come from those who have had a true encounter with God. Such experiences go beyond sacred texts, involving a real interaction with the God that provides insights and guidance for their journey.

Those with spiritual gifts will steer you away from the deceptions of unfaithful preachers and lead you to understand the true nature of God's way through Christ. It's essential to recognize that the value of life is not in material possessions, but in the creator of all. As Luke teaches, focus on seeking, understanding, and knowing me, your God, and you will no longer yearn for earthly riches. For I, your God, am the treasure you seek. Just as I created you, so have I created what you desire. Do not chase the world, for it cannot give life. Seek me, your God, the sovereign of the world.

When you seek the Lord Jesus and He becomes a part of your life, you will join the many who are indifferent to worldly judgments. Whether they travel by foot or are despised by those around them, they remain unconcerned with the devil's opinion. They have the Lord, and what more could they desire from this world? They act not on their own accord, and their understanding is not their own, but rather, it is through God's love that they perceive.

Hold the Lord near. Allow the Lord to influence your life in everything you do. Be a representation of God's presence on earth to all who seek to know Him. May you become a blessing to others, just as the Lord Jesus Christ is a blessing to everyone.

# Lesson Forty Nine

## WAIT UPON THE LORD

You are esteemed among the influential figures in the Christian faith because of your unwavering belief even in the absence of physical evidence. Unlike the disciples who had direct encounters with the Lord, you hold onto your faith without seeing. Maintain this faith as you pursue that which you desire.

The foundation of the Lord's kingdom on earth is belief. It is your faith that fortifies you as a Christian. The disciples were privileged to witness the Lord, His miracles, and His ascension to heaven. However, contemporary individuals learn of these events through scripture. Who is the stronger believer, you or the disciples? You possess more strength than you realize. Paul was exceedingly strong and will be lauded by many. He did not encounter the Lord Jesus Christ or accompany Him initially, yet he demonstrated profound understanding of the Lord's kingdom.

Belief and perseverance are key as you wait upon the Lord. Many have spent years waiting for marriage, shedding tears in the struggle. They witnessed revelations in the spiritual realm that were beyond their expectations, things they never imagined they would see due to this marriage battle. The journey was not merely about finding a spouse; it was a divine process that shaped you into who you are now.

In this struggle, the devil played a role, possessing only a limited grasp of God's plans. His power sought to undermine all that you represented, including your marriage. He consistently opposed anyone interested in you, believing your marriage was the channel through which God would be glorified. Yet, this battle was designed to mold you into a unique kind of soldier, one prepared to stand firm in future battles. Once you acquired the understanding God intended, God introduced you to a woman. You could have met her and married within five months. By the sixth month, she was expecting, and by the fourteenth month, you were celebrating the birth of a son.

satan operates like an actor following a script, yet he knows little of it. This script is authored by God and known only to Him. Unaware of the impending glory, satan adhered to this script during the crucifixion of Jesus Christ, not realizing the significance of the Lord's death and the glory to come with it.

This script delves into the origins of the prophets, tracing back to Jeremiah, who felt uncertain about the timing of his divine messages to God's people. Figures like King David, Samson, and numerous others also played pivotal roles in this spiritual lineage. It is evident that God is aware of your journey, and ultimately, one cannot evade His guiding presence.

Recognize that the divine is omniscient, and in due time, your prayers will be answered. Let us traverse this world with delight and contentment, acknowledging that our Creator has already bestowed upon us. If you have been summoned by Him, trust that He has a purpose for you. Practice patience in this journey.

# Lesson Fifty

# SATAN'S TIME IS LIMITED

As the devil's time approaches, so does the time for your enemies. While enduring hardships and questioning why your enemy persists, remember, their time is now.

Who can describe the joy when the sinful angels were cast down to earth? This joy has since turned to frustration on earth, as the devil has persistently mistreated humanity. It is known in the scriptures that the Lord Jesus Christ openly states satan's time is short, and he is acting hastily. Indeed, his time is short, and he has little time left to mislead humanity, the inheritors of the earth. The devil must realize his defeat and accept his destiny. They have nothing left to prove and no longer hold any hope in their cause. He will never replace God. He may attempt to lead man astray from God, but he will never be exalted as God is. He is not God.

The scriptures chronicle the saga of the fallen angels, noting the reverence they once held and their distinguished appearance. Despite these attributes, they yearned for more, coveting even that which was not theirs. Such envy has led humanity astray. satan has woven his trait of rebellion into mankind, diverting them from God's way. Envy, akin to the devil's, breeds hatred for those who surpass us and desire for what others possess. This led to Abel's demise and the crucifixion of Jesus Christ, all manifestations of the devil's influence.

The good news is that his time is now; there is no tomorrow. Reflect on your life in Christ. Consider how often you have implored the Lord, "For how long will my enemies harm me while you remain silent?" You have journeyed alongside those who have wronged you since they first laid eyes on you, who have levied false accusations to see you fail. You have questioned God, "Why, I hear your voice and you hear mine, you know the wrongs these people have committed against me, why are they still present?" Why must I tread the same path, sit with the same foes, when I have a mighty God who could vanquish them all? Always remember the words of the Lord Jesus regarding the fall of satan: "I saw satan fall like lightning from heaven." satan persistently erred in the Lord's presence. In Isaiah, God discusses satan's grandeur and his desire for his father's authority. This was not a brief event; it continued indefinitely. And in their hearts, everyone wondered, how long will this last? There are moments when you witness someone challenging your God, and you question; how long will this persist? How long must the devil defy his God before He laments in the scriptures, "Surely your turning of things upside down shall be esteemed as the potter's clay: for shall the work say of him that made it, he did not make me? Or shall the thing formed say of him that formed it, he lacks understanding?"

The devil, in his frustration, opposed God and all those with Him. He sought to manipulate heaven and attempted to destroy what the Lord had created. But, there is rejoicing in the devil's failures. As depicted in the scriptures, there was joy when the devil was expelled from heaven. Similarly, there will be joy among mankind on the day when satan is held accountable for his actions against humanity. On that day, God will confront satan before you and declare openly that the failures you experienced were his doing. It was because of him that you failed to have a child. It was because of him that you faced death.

Every sinful mindset originates from the devil, as was the case with Adam and Eve. Under God's influence, they lived contentedly, undisturbed by the world. However, the sinful mindset emerged, leading them to sin. Through His grace, the Lord God did not end their lives, understanding the root of sin. He offered them an opportunity to recognize Him and follow His ways. Likewise, the Lord Jesus Christ extends this opportunity to you, despite your sins. He is aware of sin's origin and does not hold you accountable if you choose to acknowledge Him and allow Him to guard you against sin.

# Lesson Fifty One

## BE HAPPY
## FOR THOSE WHO WIN

When you wait and do not obtain your desires, it's easy
to feel envious of those who have. Instead, rejoice and
celebrate their success, for your turn is coming soon.

Every person who walks this earth encounters frustration. All will struggle to attain their desires. satan tempts the desires of the faithful, seeking to undermine anything that might strengthen their faith in the Lord Jesus Christ. You may have lost your job, or the woman you intended to marry chose another. You struggle to meet your needs and must rely on what your mother provides. Your worship is fueled by the remarkable deeds you've witnessed, the wonders the Lord has performed for those around you. This inspiration sustains your belief that He will do the same for you. The unseen force that propels you forward is faith—the faith that God will fulfill His promises.

Faith in God does not rest solely on personal experiences but on the collective blessings witnessed in others' lives. When you observe your sister welcoming a child after five years of longing, your mother overcoming the grief of widowhood to live in her dream home, and your fellow worshipper celebrating new life after the heartbreak of loss, these are all affirmations that the Lord's faithfulness endures.

It's not just about His capabilities or promises; it's about your heart and your love for the Lord. Which form of worship is superior? Worshipping the Lord for the blessings you possess, or for the unexpected gifts you receive?

Failures may occur on your journey, but they serve to enlighten you and deepen your understanding of the Lord God you worship. Paul encountered the Lord Jesus himself through his opposition to Christ's church. It may seem he was alone, but this confrontation was Paul's pathway to experiencing Jesus Christ's love. Similarly, many Muslim and Buddhist individuals hold a profound love for the Lord God, firmly believing that Mohammed or Buddha is the true God. Their quest is for truth, and upon its discovery, everything else falls into place. For Paul, when he encountered Jesus Christ, the honors bestowed by the Pharisees paled in comparison to the truth he uncovered—the truth his heart longed for. He had persecuted Christians because he defended what he believed to be the one true God. Meeting Christ, he gained insight into the divine mysteries, which illuminated his understanding of past scriptures and bridged the gap to the future.

This is why you should be able to sing and give thanks to God for others, even when your own life seems like a failure. For it is written, "The children of the desolate woman are more numerous than those of the woman who has a husband." Through others, God's power is revealed. The Lord Jesus Christ demonstrated who He was to the world through the miracles He performed. These miracles were not salvation itself but a sign that God has come and is present. My hope is for the Lord to encounter you today, to grant the desires of your heart, and for you to know what is written. As you long for it, know that the God who created everything around you is with you and cares for you.

# Lesson Fifty Two

## LOVE THE SINNERS

Do not despise those in sin, for you hate their sinful acts.
Instead, love the sinners, for redemption is
available to every person in sin.

Jesus sacrificed himself for your sins, encompassing not only those committed after his time but also by all generations past and those yet to come upon this earth. He proclaimed, "Had Sodom and Gomorrah witnessed my arrival, they surely would not have perished." Moreover, he imparted, "I leave you with peace, not as the world provides, but my own peace."

Jesus' sacrifice was for all sins, past and future. He foresaw what was to come and offered redemption through His blood. No sin outweighs this sacrifice. He bore the burden of disease, acts of homosexuality, and even murder upon the cross. Therefore, in this life, no one should label you a sinner. Invoking His name purifies and renews. He understood the world's frailties, which is why you hold a special place in His heart. He recognizes your struggles against darkness and acknowledges the devil's attempts to lead you astray. But, He assures us that by looking to the cross, where He took upon every affliction, we find salvation. In His name, we are freed from sin. Do not judge the world that has not yet experienced the love of Christ. Instead, love the world as your God loves it. Accept their sins as if they were your own. Invite all of God's people to come to Him. What they have done is of less importance. He loves them regardless. It is through human weakness that God manifests His strength, for the world to honor His name. He transforms those you had given up on. He transformed you; were you not the worst? He will transform all who believe and trust in Him.

# Lesson Fifty Three

## SPIRITUAL GROWTH IS GRADUAL

Spiritual growth is a journey fraught with challenges for those pursuing righteousness. In the struggle to avoid reverting to one's former ways, there is a constant battle against the devil who seeks to drag you back to the remnants of a sinful past.

Occasionally, one might reflect on the crucifixion and the blood that was shed. It is widely known that Jesus Christ was crucified and that he wept on the cross. Yet, why proceed with life as if this knowledge of Christ is insignificant?

This is the life of all people before they come to know God. The Lord Jesus Christ is like a conversation in a tunnel for those without hope. You recall the name of Jesus as if it were a brief news item. Afterwards, life goes on and finds its own peace. However, a day will come when keeping pace with the Lord Jesus Christ will be a struggle. Everything will begin to make sense, and you will regret the life you once lived. You will realize that the Lord Jesus Christ died for you, and you will wonder how to repay Him. He died for you, yet you remain in sin? You are aware of His grace, but find it difficult to stay away from sin. You continue to do the things you did before knowing Him, filled with regret, now that you understand sin. You strive to live a life that God desires. You will pray fervently, pleading for God's mercy. You will seek the love that brought Him into this world. You will implore the Lord to purify you and give you strength to overcome the temptations that draw you back to the sin you despise.

Transforming from sin to righteousness is not an easy journey; it is a divine process guided by God. When others seem slow to transform, it's not a matter of speed but of being in the midst of the process. As individuals learn more about God and grow in faith, many weaknesses are left behind. The devil persistently tries to lure one back to past sins, but the growth in understanding God's kingdom—and God Himself— equips one with the strength to resist temptation through the Holy Spirit's power. The battles we face are often beyond our understanding, but over time, habits fade. One may realize months later that old desires have diminished. This is the work of God, who alone comprehends the spiritual realm and operates on His own timeline, beyond our urgency.

# Lesson Fifty Four

# WE WERE CREATED WITH LOVE

Observe the myriad creations surrounding you and witness the power of your God. Each of these creations reflects the love of your God. You are a masterpiece of love, and the Lord is by your side because He cares for you.

The love of God has been with you from the beginning. You were created in love, a love that is evident in the perfection of creation visible to mankind. Observe your surroundings and the other creatures that journey alongside you; surely, this is a testament to creation made in love. Jesus Christ spoke of His love for humanity, likening you to the birds of the air that neither sow nor reap nor gather into barns, yet are provided for. Consider the flowers of the field that do not toil or spin. What then of you, whom He loves dearly? He has bestowed upon you the ability to understand and communicate with Him. Surely, the Lord will do much more for you.

This is a question every person should ponder: Can the God who created you in a world that provides for every need, fail to take care of you? When you are thirsty, there is water He created. When you are hungry, there is food—ample food to satisfy your hunger. Can He fail to take care of you?

You have lost your way with God, dedicating your lives to the pursuit of wealth. You devote time to studies that do not enrich your spiritual life. Some seek ways to recreate man, neglecting the search for man's creator. Worldly desires have distanced you from your God, as you begin to idolize the material world. Cars and wealth have become objects of worship, to the extent of committing heinous acts for them. It is a deviation from God that marks your failure.

God's love for Man remains as steadfast as it was at creation. This love, embodied in the sacrifice of the Lord Jesus Christ who died for all, is the love I wish to convey in my writing to you. It is available to all who seek it. God is not hidden; He promises that those who seek Him will find Him. He is not concealed in deserts or forests, necessitating the moving of mountains to discover Him. He is present with you at this moment, desiring for you to feel His presence. While you have pursued wealth, perhaps it is time to seek the path to your God.

The Lord God descended to Earth so that all humanity might know and comprehend Him. He expressed Himself clearly for us to observe and grasp His identity. Foreseeing the future and aware of satan's designs for the world, He provided a way to escape the devil's influence, and it is this way that I present to you at this moment.

The Lord exists as depicted in the scriptures. He speaks as clearly as when he traversed the streets of Galilee and Jerusalem. He communicates with many, and they hear his voice. He shares what he cherishes about the world and what displeases him. Daily, he walks alongside them, revealing sights unseen by their eyes alone. He has exposed the animosity of one man towards another. He has revealed how the world, considering itself progressive, has regressed to the days of Babylon, Sodom, and Gomorrah. He has shown his displeasure with mankind and the religious leaders who remain silent on sin.

*"I AM the Lord your God; I began this world with Israel, my cherished nation. Israel endured nothing that I did not foresee. It was for the world. Through Israel, I sacrificed men for your sake. Through Israel, I performed miracles so all nations could witness my might and not equate me with*

*any other gods. I entered this world and revealed myself to everyone out of love. I cherish the world, for I am its creator. You are all my people, diverse in color, and your beauty reflects my love, the Lord your God. Yet, you have strayed from my love, pursuing selfish desires. You dismiss my words and doubt my command. You consider yourselves wiser and greater than I, your God. I AM the Lord your God, and I call you to return to me. When you do, I will absolve all your transgressions."*

# TEACH PEOPLE TO KNOW GOD

People need to learn to pray and your work as a clergy, pastor or priest is to teach God's people how to reach him. When you teach a man to pray, you teach a man to know and love God. For when a man was brought a woman, he learnt of a woman, and he loved to be with that woman. Prayer brings man close to God and God teaches man to love him.

The most effective method of prayer and worship involves incorporating your personal circumstances into songs or scriptures. Through these scriptures, I aim to impart the essence of true worship, as reflected in the words I've written. These words align with the proper way to worship. While many hymns are crafted for congregational singing, the primary focus should be personal; it is you who seeks a breakthrough, it is you who needs the Lord. In Jinja, there was a church where the sermon centered on instructing people in prayer. Remarkably, not a single preacher in that church embraced the sermon. The message criticized the clergy for not teaching congregants how to pray effectively, accusing them of prioritizing attendance and offerings over spiritual empowerment, especially during nocturnal spiritual challenges.

The scriptures in this book highlight the significance of worshipping through hymns whenever one feels spiritually attacked. The Lord is attentive and responds to all who reach out in prayer or worship. It is essential for people to understand the essence of true worship. Advancing God's work can be greatly furthered by selflessly sharing your gifts. Seeking control over every aspect is not advisable. Aspiring to be the only leader of the worship team, the singular reference for God's word, and the sole authority on prayer can be restrictive for both oneself and others. Because of your selfishness and evil desires, you force tangs in your mouth to seek authority.

God is the Word, and His Word is for all His people. Such selfishness is why some refuse to welcome those who appear more anointed, fearing they will attract the congregation's following. This leads to God's messengers being turned away from churches. The Lord Jesus Christ commands, "Go into all the world and preach the gospel to every creature." The intent should be for each to teach another, yet churches have become battlegrounds rather than places of learning God's Word. Preachers are disparaged from the pulpit without cause. Christians  should not be part of a congregation where preachers disparage one another. Serving in the unified body of Christ, it is He who organizes His house. Continual blame from the pulpit leaves little time to tend to the congregation. Focus on preaching God's word, and He will guide the lost to the right path.

Though He has commanded you to spread the gospel throughout the world, He  precedes you in all your endeavors. You cannot preach without His grace. Just as He has said that the poor will always be among us, so too will false prophets exist until the end of time. Proclaim God's word and prove yourselves to be His true disciples. Those who seek Him will evaluate you based on His deeds through you and His words from your lips. If He can draw near those sinners who do not seek Him, those in shrines worshipping idols, then what of the lost sheep that seeks Him but has been deceived by a false prophet? He will certainly find them and reveal to them the true signs that they are in the wrong place.

Jesus preached on this earth, speaking less of false prophets, yet was labeled as such by many. Are you certain that the message you've received is from the Lord and confirms the preacher you denounce is false? Instruct God's people about His kingdom. Intercede for His flock, that they may not wander. Guide them in worship, in prayer, and in combating darkness. Educate them about God's realm so they can disseminate His word as He instructed. Let every person know God intimately and understand how to rightfully call upon their Father. As they come to know their God, they will discern false teachings. For when you believe in the Lord Jesus Christ, He and the Father will come to you. With their arrival, you will recognize the darkness, for their light is with you, and where there is light, darkness cannot prevail.

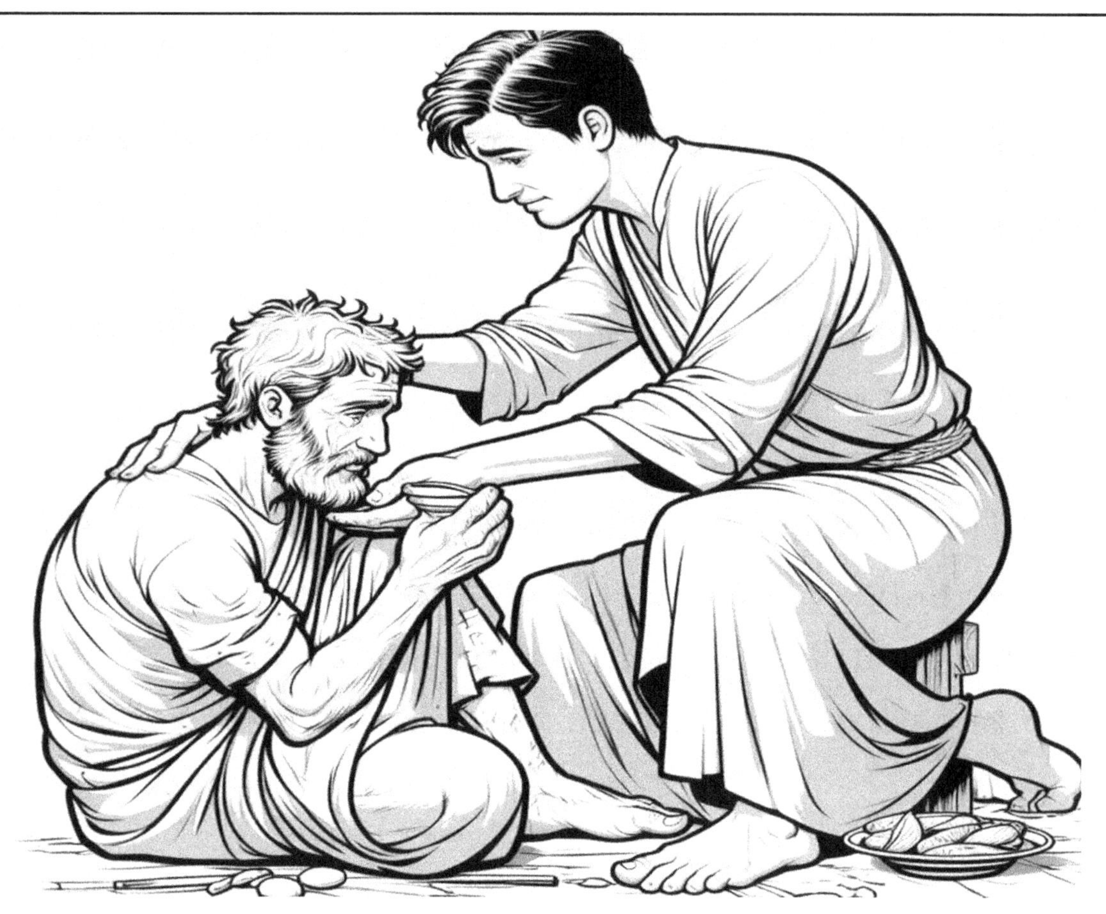

# Lesson Fifty Six

# SUPPORT EACH OTHER

In unity with Christ, support one another, especially during times of failure. Why subject your brethren to earthly judges when the righteous stumble into sin? The Lord Jesus Christ sent His Spirit to address the frailties of His followers. He alone is the judge of his flock, not the corrupt legal systems that pass judgment on his people.

Fear not the devil, his power, nor his name. You have been chosen by God to shepherd His flock and guide them. He has bestowed upon you the authority to cast out all evil from His people. Even as satan strives to weaken you with his deeds that have led man astray, declare with conviction, "I shall overcome all."God will fortify you with strength, both day and night, to confront the wickedness that blocks your way.

As a follower of the Lord Jesus Christ, you will face battles until your final day. satan's goal is for you to perish in sin. Sin pervades this world, often appearing where least expected. Choosing to follow the Lord Jesus Christ sets you at odds with satan. Being anointed with great abilities by the Holy Spirit  makes you a target, a proving ground for the devil to challenge your worthiness of that anointing, to show you are no different from him. Remember Peter, who denied Jesus three times; Abraham, who fathered a child with his wife's servant; King David, who committed murder and adultery; and Solomon, who turned to idol worship.

Jesus' words to Peter were, "satan has asked to sift you as wheat." While Jesus speaks little of this request, we can draw parallels with the story of Job. satan often compares himself to God's chosen, unable to comprehend how a lesser creation like man can resist his temptations and not succumb to his faults. Peter stumbled, just as David, Abraham, and Solomon did before him, and just as anyone can falter today. However, what is crucial is who stands by you in both failure and success.

Jesus was aware that Peter would falter, yet also that he would recover.

He understood that he would be present to lift Peter up, for he knew the nature of Peter's heart. However, humans have often failed to support one another. It is crucial to recognize the devil's attempts to dishonor the Lord Jesus Christ. The evil committed in the Lord's name brings not shame upon oneself, but upon the Lord Himself.

Some time ago, the former Archbishop of the Church of Uganda was dismissed from his duties due to adultery. This act is condemned by Jesus. Recall the biblical story of the woman caught in adultery who was about to be stoned to death? The pivotal moment in this narrative isn't the men discarding their stones and acknowledging their own sins as they leave; it's the words Jesus spoke to the woman. He asked, "Woman, where are they? Has no one condemned you?" She replied, "No one, sir." Jesus then said, "Neither do I condemn you. Go now and leave your life of sin."

"The statement 'Neither do I condemn you' holds immense power in this narrative. While adultery is a sin, on this earth, God condemns no one. So why do we condemn each other? Why does the church shame its own for sinning? Our purpose is to embrace sinners, as commanded by our Lord. Being a bishop does not equate to being God; he is human. It is not recorded that King David was stripped of his kingship or denounced by God when he committed adultery, nor was Abraham, Peter, or Solomon. So why should you be? Support one another as followers of Jesus Christ. Be aware that the devil is relentless. Reclaim your brothers before they are entirely lost. As Paul stated, it is impossible for those who have been enlightened, who have tasted the heavenly gift, who have partaken in the Holy Spirit , who have savored the goodness of God's word and the powers of the coming age, if they fall away, to be brought back to repentance. By falling away, they are crucifying the Son of God all over again and subjecting him to public disgrace."

The reason is that the devil has tested such men's wrath when they served God. Once they fall, he will battle to prevent them from seeing the light again. Many will perish in sin prematurely. Therefore, it is crucial to recognize the significant effort of our Lord in enabling Peter, David, Solomon, Abraham, and others to stand again. These men experienced the Lord's goodness, fell, but were later raised by the Lord. One should not leave them to battle alone. Through the power of the Holy Spirit, God has entrusted you with the responsibility to fight for others. Do not blame anyone for their sins, but strive to win them back.

# Lesson Fifty Seven

# THE BLOOD OF JESUS

**Can you grasp the significance of Jesus' blood in human salvation? What is the implication of the Lord's blood serving as a sacrifice for humanity? Was this sacrifice accepted by the devil?**

The concept of God's grace is subject to various interpretations by those who study the scriptures. Some view this grace as God's choice to sacrifice Himself for man's sins. Others perceive grace in the suffering and degradation He endured from His creations, and still others, in the authority of His name over darkness. However, the aspect that has perplexed many is "the blood of Jesus Christ." Discussions about the blood of Jesus Christ abound, but the specific phrase, "With my blood, you will fight the power of the darkness," is not directly quoted in the scriptures. The significance of Jesus' blood lies in its role as a symbol of life and sacrifice, pivotal to the Christian faith.

In the scriptures, it is said that the Lord Jesus Christ proclaimed, "I am the lamb," which symbolizes "the sacrifice." Jesus represents the ultimate sacrifice for man's sins. He became the enduring substitute for the sacrificial lambs offered by man. The question then arises: how does the Lord's blood gain significance in combating darkness?

The Lord's blood was offered as a ransom for the debt of sin, not as a demand from the devil to abandon His people. From the beginning, the Lord required sacrifice as a sign of repentance to pardon His people's sins. It wasn't that the Lord God consumed the lambs and cows; rather, the act of sacrifice was a human acknowledgment of wrongdoing and a desire to remain in God's grace. God is aware of the world humans inhabit and the constant malevolent influence from fallen angels, making mankind susceptible to error. The blood of Jesus established a New Covenant, signifying that when His people seek Him through His blood, He will absolve their sins, regardless of the sin's magnitude. The Lord has chosen to offer forgiveness.

In the struggle against darkness, we reflect on the death of the Lord Jesus Christ. The Lord's death was not caused by human power but was prophesied in the scriptures and fulfilled on the cross. Although God orchestrated this event, He is not associated with evil. Instead, it was satan who undertook the evil act of crucifying Jesus. This serves as a reminder that where there is light, darkness also lurks. Jesus was aware of satan's plot against Him. From His birth, targeted by King Herod, to the betrayal by Judas, instigated by the Pharisees, these were all indications of the devil's plan for Jesus's demise. The scriptures state clearly that when Judas accepted the bread, satan entered him. Thus, Jesus said to him, "What you are going to do, do quickly," addressing satan, not Judas. This illustrates that where God is present, so is the devil. It is a caution to all who consider themselves holy. For those who deny the existence of satan, be aware that he is present and opposes Godly deeds. The death of Jesus was under the devil's influence, characterized by anger, envy, hatred, and the unjust decision to exchange Him for a sinner. The devil orchestrated the crucifixion of Jesus, fulfilling the scriptures as ordained by God. When Jesus was led to the cross, it was the devil who was responsible for shedding His blood. Therefore, Jesus pleaded, "Father, forgive them, for they do not know what they are doing." He asked for forgiveness because it was the devil at work. I teach that when the devil assails you, remind him of Jesus's blood, which he caused to be shed. What more could he want from you? He was present during Jesus's suffering, aware of His identity, yet allowed His blood to be spilled for you.

When God accepted sacrifices as described by Moses, He pardoned their sins. Jesus proclaimed loudly, and the devil heard, "Just as the Father knows me and I know the Father, I lay down my life for the sheep." John bears witness, saying, "Look, the Lamb of God, who takes away the sin of the world!" The devil acknowledged the lamb and aided in the shedding of its blood for the people. He requires nothing from man and holds no sway over them, whether they are in sin or not. The Lord God is the deity of all humanity. Through that blood, God redeems the wicked and renders them righteous. And when you call upon Him, He will surely answer, at no further cost, for He has paid it all.

Lesson Fifty Eight

# LET'S LEARN TO WAIT

Don't feel disheartened if you haven't yet experienced
your breakthrough. Everything worthwhile comes
through waiting. Consider Abraham's 100-year wait for a
son or Jacob's 14 years of hard work. In hindsight,
you'll see that it wasn't just waiting but a
journey of personal growth.

After a long period of bachelorhood, a man found a woman he wished to marry. He decided to introduce her to his mother officially. On their way back, a heavy rain began, obscuring his view while driving. He contemplated stopping the car but continued on. Suddenly, he felt a message from the Holy Spirit, a reminder of the victory he had just achieved. For the first time in 17 years, he had introduced a woman to his mother as his future wife. He interpreted the rain as a symbol of overcoming the devil's opposition. Inspired, he received a song from the Holy Spirit , 'Weebale Mukama Weebale' (Thank You God).

Discussing spiritual warfare can cast a new light on many of your experiences. This is because God engages in different battles for various reasons. Everyone has a particular weakness that the devil exploits to undermine the Lord's presence in their lives. For this man, it might be marriage; for others, it could be infertility. For Abraham, it was the desire for a son; for Jacob, it was his love for Rachel; and for Joseph, it was his brothers' envy. A common thread in these scriptural accounts is the act of waiting on the Lord. Abraham waited 100 years for Isaac, Jacob waited 14 years, and this man waited 17 years to marry. It's crucial to trust in the Lord, believing that He will act in His perfect timing.

When you attend church, you may be promised miracles. Yet, the Lord Jesus questioned, "This woman has waited for 12 years; is it wrong to heal her on the Sabbath?" In the scriptures, Jesus' miracles appear to occur suddenly, leading to the expectation that when you pray or are prayed for, it will be answered immediately. Jesus indicated that the man was blind so that today, the Lord's name might be glorified. What Jesus meant was that the man had been waiting for this day when the Lord's name would be exalted.

Prayer and patience in the Lord are essential. The path to heaven is narrow, and few remain on it. There are many distractions in this world that can lead one astray from the Lord's path. When God heals, the healing is everlasting. He is the God whose name is exalted by all of creation. He must perform good works in your life before bestowing upon you what He has prepared for you.

Abraham journeyed from his ancestral land; Moses abandoned the splendors of Egyptian royalty to be humbled before encountering the burning bush. David tended flocks, even with God's promise through the prophet Samuel, he waited. Continue to wait, for God is aware of your path and is preparing you for His glory. Strive for heaven; it is the ultimate goal. Your faith lies in patience, and this patience is your battle. Whether in rain or sunshine, remain steadfast with the Lord.

# THE GOOD DO SUFFER

Why give in to sadness when your prayers appear to go unanswered? Despite your heartfelt prayers, challenges have persisted. You have experienced the pain of losing a child and your spouse fighting cancer. Suffering is not limited to the sinful, even the righteous face trials. As your faith strengthens, you will realize that the righteous often carry heavier burdens than the unrighteous.

One day, a man brought his ailing brother to fellowship. His brother had been sick for several days, grew weak, and eventually passed away. Before his death, the man worshipped and prayed fervently, hoping God would answer his prayers and heal his brother. He sang of a steadfast God, present in both joy and sorrow. Despite his devout praise and faith, his brother did not recover. This left him and others who believed in his spiritual gift puzzled as to why his brother was not  healed. Their grief mirrored the sorrow in the scriptures when Lazarus died; if Jesus could cure a man's blindness, why not save Lazarus? Yet, the same scriptures remind us that God "causes His sun to rise on the evil and the good, and sends rain on the righteous and the unrighteous."

Who says that only sinners shall die? "God takes not just the sinners, but the faithful as well." This should be a lesson to all. Suffering does not solely befall sinners. Elisha, who was without sin, succumbed to disease and pain. The challenge within the church is the expectation that the faithful will not suffer. There's a belief that God's anointed should embody wealth and prosperity. Preachers think they are judged more by their physical possessions than by their unseen qualities. Yet, our Lord Jesus was physically impoverished. He had no chariots like the Romans, no homes, nor buildings. He traveled by foot until the day he ascended to heaven. How can you represent God if you are assessed by your wealth? Prophet Samuel, too, traveled on foot, yet he bore the most potent messages for both King David and Saul.

When called to serve God, humility comes naturally. Physical wealth is seen as the ground beneath your feet, accompanying you wherever you go. Why contend for something you believe is already yours? This echoes David's sentiment that with God, wealth is abundant and follows you without struggle. True wealth is the capacity to find joy even in physical poverty. This is embodied in the Lord Jesus Christ, which is what you represent.

## THE ASPIRATION TO EMBODY THE LORD'S HEAVENLY IMAGE ON EARTH HAS LED MANY TO BE LABELED AS SINNERS.

You have become false prophets, lacking understanding and devoid of any grace from the Holy Spirit . Adorning yourselves in white robes to mimic heavenly angels and constructing golden churches, you have ultimately fallen into idolatry.

In your work, embody humility as a follower of Jesus Christ. You Worship a humble God who instills hope in the poor. Their hope lies not in these earthly possessions but in heaven. Avoid leading them astray from heaven with earthly possessions. Find joy in the salvation that the Lord imparts through you to His children. Rejoice in having less, for the Lord teaches, seek the kingdom of heaven first, and all else shall be added unto you.

## Lesson Sixty

# GOD SPEAKS IN DREAM

What you dream, it's not what you saw before you slept.
God speaks in dreams and he speaks that exactly you
need to hear. Pay close attention to your dreams and ask
the Lord if you fail to remember or understand.

Disbelief in dreams and their undervaluation can be limiting. It's important to recognize that numerous songs and scriptures have originated from dreams experienced during sleep. Although dreams may be discussed in church, they often go ignored or are misunderstood by those who do listen. Accepting the Lord into one's life is accompanied by dreaming, which signifies a new form of communication with the Lord God. Recording your dreams can often reveal a profound message from the Lord.

You might doubt my words if I talk about singing and walking in dreams. However, God grants gifts to each individual uniquely. In the same way, He communicates with His children through various means. Many instances that have strengthened your faith in Christ have their roots in the spiritual world. Joseph's power was in his capacity to dream and decipher dreams. Just as the scriptures refer to "speaking in tongues," it also pertains to dreams. Only God has the authority to interpret these dreams, not man. The devil is oblivious to your dreams until you recall them. It is only those dreams that God allows that can be comprehended while dreaming. The devil becomes aware of your dreams when you remember them after waking. Such is the formidable power of spirits that they can read your thoughts, swaying your everyday actions.

When you dream and then forget, it might be an act of God or satan. Some forget their dreams because the devil intends to prevent the message within from being received. The devil is believed to have the power to erase knowledge from your mind, particularly if the dream conveys a message of salvation. Therefore, if you frequently forget your dreams, it is advised to pray for the removal of any spirit that may be taking them. As you deepen your service to the Lord, the devil may take an interest in your thoughts, words, and dreams. Similarly, the Lord might prevent you from remembering a dream, similar to the situation with John the Baptist's birth. Zechariah's speech was taken away to protect the news of John's birth from enemies. Recalling a dream can make you vulnerable to these enemies. However, once John was born, Zechariah's speech was restored. In time, when the dream is realized, you will recall it and share with others that you had dreamt of this event.

## Lesson Sixty One

# ONE FAILURE IS NOT THAT GOD HAS FAILED

Experiencing failure can lead to the belief that the Lord has also failed us, casting doubt on our ability to achieve what we seek. However, often what we fail at is not crucial to our success. Where you failed was a segment of your success that the Lord had set to be a failure.

In the wake of disappointment and feelings of failure, you find yourself questioning God's identity. Is He truly the Savior He claims to be, capable of altering any circumstance?

In worship and praise, it's common to find oneself questioning God through hymns. 'Tell me about Lord Jesus? What is His story? Is He the one who died for me? Is He the one who promised to answer when I pray? Yet, I have just lost a battle. Why wasn't He there?' This is a mindset many adopt after experiencing failure, openly lamenting that the Lord has allowed them to be shamed and the devil to triumph. But you don't believe in defeat; you know that the devil cannot prevail because of the God you worship.

A man came to the realization that he had lost his battle to wed. Standing on his office balcony, he whispered to his heart, "The devil has triumphed." Indeed, his face bore all the marks of defeat. He returned home, sat by his door, and wept. His tears were not for the loss of the woman he loved, but because he believed satan had stripped him of his strength, challenging the notion that God never fails. For what had been divinely bestowed upon him was now gone. Did this imply that God was weak, or a deceiver? No, there was an aspect he failed to comprehend.

Reflect on the story of Moses and his encounters with the Pharaoh of Egypt. Despite numerous pleas, the Pharaoh consistently refused. Consider Moses, who had faith in the might of his God and the certainty that His words would manifest instantly. This aspect is often neglected in one's struggle against evil. It is believed that when God speaks, it cannot falter. Yet, there are times when He may say one thing but intend another.

God sent Moses, knowing Pharaoh would resist, yet Moses was unaware. As a man, he could only lament to the Lord, "You have allowed Pharaoh to prevail." In time, God disclosed to Moses, "I will harden Pharaoh's heart." There were divine reasons for Moses to confront Pharaoh with ten plagues, and with a single command, he parted the sea. Our existence is not solely for personal gain but for the benefit of all God's creation. God cannot be concealed for oneself; He must be witnessed by all. The plagues demonstrated the might of the God of Israel to the world. They earned the Israelites respect wherever they journeyed. Nations proclaimed to the Israelites, "We have heard of what your God did to the Egyptians."

What I impart to you is that God's battles are not solely for those who know Him, but also for all who will hear of how the Lord triumphed in your struggles. What more do I teach? Not everything will unfold as promised. Our minds are too limited to grasp the full scope. When Jesus says, "I am coming soon," we glance at the clock, our thoughts too constrained to envision beyond. The devil may take what the Lord has granted you. Yet, the real question is: which battle are you engaged in? Is it to win over a specific person, or is it to achieve marriage? The true battle lies in the pursuit of marriage, and it is there that satan holds you captive.

Focusing on a specific woman or man who breaks your heart may lead you to believe that marriage is unattainable. Even if another person also breaks your heart, remember that the struggle isn't about finding the most beautiful or handsome partner; it's about the journey towards marriage itself.

A man prayed for a partner and was shown a small, slender girl in his dreams, whom he learned was named Ankunda. After three dreams, he believed she was destined to be his wife. Despite searching, he couldn't find her until one day, she entered the church and sat next to him. As they prayed together, holding hands, he recognized her as the woman from his visions. During the following service, she indicated a desire to talk. They spoke and found joy in each other's company. However, over time, her feelings seemed to change, and eventually, she disappeared from his life. Despite this, he remained convinced that she was the one God had revealed to him as his wife, yet her whereabouts remained unknown.

The battle was about marriage, not a woman. Let this be a lesson in all the battles you engage in. The devil may take away what you believe God has given you. But was it ever a part of the battle, or genuinely given? Moses approached Pharaoh with confidence, turning a stick into a snake, believing Pharaoh would free the Israelites. Yet, he returned disappointed. How many challenges must you overcome to receive what you've prayed for? You cannot know, but God understands why He chooses such battles. Those who know and trust in Him bear witness to His greatness and power to the world.

# Lesson Sixty Two

# LET'S TEACH PEOPLE HOW TO REACH GOD

Your failure to educate people on how to connect with God has led to the rise of false prophets. Consequently, many Christians with limited scriptural knowledge accept everything these false prophets say as truth.

Awoman was given a message for her brother. Guided by the Holy Spirit , she was instructed on how he should worship during a challenging time in his life when he needed the strength to persevere. The message was clear: "Tell him to sing hymn 333 (Omukwano Gwa Yesu/Loved with everlasting love), and in the second verse, to lay down the troubles he is facing." This guidance was not just a message, but a legacy to be handed down through generations. Henceforth, he applied these instructions to every hymn he sang.

In reading the written scriptures, one finds a gap; among all the teachings, none instruct man on how to pray. A man shared his testimony, saying, "One day, as I sifted through documents in a folder, I stumbled upon a page titled 'forbidden books.' Curious about the contents, I discovered writings from a cult. The document detailed methods of meditating with evil spirits, providing step-by-step instructions on where to stand, how to draw symbols, where to gaze, and what incantations to utter."

The Bible scriptures do not explicitly detail the prayers of Peter, Matthew, and John. Despite their close relationship with Jesus and their experiences with the Holy Spirit, the manner in which they prayed is not documented. This absence leaves modern Christians without specific scriptural guidance on prayer and worship. It appears that the compilers of the Bible omitted these potentially instructive scriptures that could teach individuals how to pray to God.

For this reason, church leaders have grown so influential that many believe only they can pray in a way that God will listen. They alone, it is thought, can read the Bible and comprehend God's Word. Indeed, God has historically chosen specific individuals to carry out His work, such as prophets and apostles. However, this does not preclude others from learning to pray. The scriptures recount in Daniel that an angel told him, "Do not fear, Daniel, for from the first day you set your heart to understand and humbled yourself before your God, your words were heard, and I have come in response to them. But the prince of the Persian kingdom resisted me for twenty-one days. Then Michael, one of the chief princes, came to assist me, because I was detained there with the kings of Persia."

Daniel gained the Lord's attention through his fervent prayers, which were answered. There is a method of prayer that elicits a response from the Lord, and it involves using His word. God's word serves as His covenant, and it is crucial to remind Him of His promises. Everything documented in the scriptures represents God's word and His commitments to humanity. The events described in the scriptures demonstrate the Lord's power. He has assured you that if you believe, you can achieve even greater things. The Lord's power extends beyond His depiction in the scriptures. To receive what you need from Him, you must learn to pray correctly, utilizing His word in both worship and supplication.

The initial lesson is that you are the focus of His word. In Luke, Jesus declares, "Behold, I give unto you the power to tread on serpents and scorpions, and over all the power of the enemy: and nothing shall by any means harm you." This verse can be employed in two ways: to rebuke the devil or to invoke the Lord and remind Him of the authority He has granted you. This word is given to you; use it for your protection.

One morning, a man awoke to a face he had never seen before staring directly at him. It was an unfamiliar spirit. He rebuked it, yet it continued to smile at him until it vanished. By afternoon, he felt a weakness overtaking his body, realizing he was under attack. A chill unlike any other spread through him, deep within his bones, unreachable and piercing like the cold of a lake at midnight. His back ached, preventing him from sitting or standing still for even thirty seconds. Knowing he was under attack, he turned to worship and prayer, singing hymns that he believed would summon God's presence. Despite this, the pain intensified. Unable to kneel, he lay on the couch, pleading with God, "You promised protection, so why this pain? In Luke, you granted me authority over the darkness, so why this attack?" He continued to question and worship until sleep claimed him. Upon awakening, he found himself completely healed.

Such is the power of God's word. Remind Him of His promises, and He will not fail to heal you. For His word represents His covenant and standing with man and all of creation. He will never allow it to be disgraced.

# Lesson Sixty Three

# HOW TO OPEN A SERVICE

Let's learn the ways to reach God and find his blessings. There are specific ways in which God wishes things to be done, and when followed as He desires, He bestows abundant blessings. The way the Lord desires you to pray, the same he desires you to learn and understand how to pray to him.

In this book, it is emphasized that without God, nothing is achievable, be it worship or prayer. It highlights the devil's intent to destroy and the necessity to call upon God under all circumstances to counteract the devil's malign influence. Learning the correct way to pray is crucial. Many church leaders begin services with a worship song followed by a prayer, often recited from a common prayer book. However, what is often overlooked is the importance of inviting the Holy Spirit. No church service should commence without a dedicatory prayer to invite the Holy Spirit , as the battle is against forces beyond human comprehension that despise worship and prayer. Inviting the angels and the Holy Spirit  is essential to worship God without interruption.

*TO OPEN A SERVICE IN PRAYER, ONE OFFERS THANKS TO GOD, SEEKS REPENTANCE, DEDICATES THE SERVICE, AND INVITES THE PRESENCE OF ANGELS AND THE HOLY SPIRIT .*

## -----> LET'S THANK THE LORD

Almighty Father, the architect of the celestial and terrestrial realms, we express our gratitude for your boundless love, compassion, and benevolence. Our appreciation extends to all your deeds, both known and unknown to us. We are thankful for the gift of life, enabling us to gather today and offer worship and adoration to your name. Your provision, sustenance, healing touch, and nurturing care are acknowledged with heartfelt thanks. We are especially grateful for the lives of our children and your unwavering love and guidance in every aspect of our lives. We recognize and appreciate your protective hand, shielding us in times of adversity and thwarting the schemes of the adversary. Your victory over the forces of darkness is a testament to your supremacy and our ultimate triumph.

# -----> START REPENTING

Let us repent our sins - Heavenly Father, we approach you in repentance of our sins. We acknowledge we are unworthy of your presence, even to gaze upon the crumbs from your table. We have sinned; we lie, we kill, we destroy. We commit adultery, we harbor hatred, and we tarnish the Image you found pleasing on the day of our creation. Our eyes have beheld what they should not, our tongues have spoken forbidden words, our hands have touched the untouchable, and our feet have trodden forbidden paths. Heavenly Father, grant us forgiveness. In accordance with the promise you made through your prophet Moses, lend your ear to our prayers and your gaze to our afflictions. Absolve us of our ancestors' transgressions, and let not their sins haunt us or our descendants. We also repent for our enemies; Lord, forgive them, for they know less what they do.

# -----> LET'S DEDICATE

Let's consecrate the service - Heavenly Father, we commit this day into your care. We call your mercy, strength, and dominion over us sevenfold, 1,2,3,4,5,6, 7 times by the power of the Holy Spirit, in the name of the

Lord Jesus Christ. Lord Jesus, You granted us this dominion in Luke, saying, "I have given you authority to tread upon serpents and scorpions and over all the enemy's might; nothing shall by any means hurt you." Lord God, with this dominion, we rebuke every force of darkness within this assembly. We summon your encircling flames of protection around this church sevenfold 1,2,3,4,5,6,7 times by the power of the Holy Spirit, in the name of the Lord Jesus Christ. We consecrate and protect this church with your blood sevenfold 1,2,3,4,5,6,7 times by the power of the Holy Spirit, in the name of our Lord Jesus Christ.

# -----> LET'S INVITE

Now, let us welcome the Holy Spirit and the Holy Angels. - Dear God, in the book of Matthew, you granted us the key. You commanded that whatever we open in heaven shall be opened on earth. Lord Jesus, Using that key, we open your eyes to see us and witness the suffering we endure. We open your eyes to recognize all the adversaries that stand against us. We open your ears to hear our prayers and our praise on this day. We open your legs to halt all the evil that seeks to assail us. And Lord, we open your hands to bestow upon us all that we need and petition for. We open the heavens sevenfold 1,2,3,4,5,6,7 times by the power of the Holy Spirit, in the name of our Lord Jesus Christ. We summon the angels of protection to shield us from all wickedness. We call upon the angel of praise to help us worship you as you truly deserve. We invite all your angels to join us as we exalt your name. We call upon you, the Holy Spirit, to ensure all we do today aligns with your will. May you lead us throughout this service until its conclusion. We offer this prayer through the power of the Holy Spirit, in the name of our Lord Jesus Christ, Amen.

## *THIS PRAYER IS A PRAYER TO HELP ALL MAN REACH THE LORD GOD IN THE HEAVENS. THE LORD GOD LISTENS WHEN MAN PRAYS BUT THE LORD IS PLEASED WHEN MAN PRAYS RIGHTLY.*

Scriptures are intended to guide man in understanding how to connect swiftly with their God. However, many have not mastered these texts well enough to utilize them in prayer.

This prayer is crucial for teaching you the correct use of scriptures in seeking the Lord God. God cherishes man and delights when people learn the proper way to communicate with Him. The purpose of mankind's existence on earth is to understand the ways of God and to comprehend the Lord's character, thus avoiding the snares of the devil. The devil, having failed to grasp the nature of his Creator, became sin itself—a sin not only to himself but to all of creation.

Man should steer clear of such pitfalls and strive to understand and worship their God as is truly deserves. This is the core purpose behind the writing of the Bible and all holy scriptures: to provide insights into the lives of those who walked with the divine and to comprehend the divine ways. This knowledge prepares one for the eventual time of unity with God.

But man has failed to comprehend his God, as the devil has infiltrated mankind, introducing forms of worship not ordained by the Lord God. This influence has altered your paths, diminishing your understanding of the Lord God whom you worship.

May this book guide you in understanding your God. May it instruct you in the ways of true worship. May it show you how to pray and pass down this prayer through generations. For this prayer contains all that is necessary to communicate with the Lord. It is a prayer bestowed by God upon His people, to aid humanity in reaching Him correctly amidst life's dark challenges. This is the Lord's Prayer, and those who pray with these words will be heard by the Lord God.

# Lesson Sixty Four

## PRAY FOR GOD'S GIFTS

God bestows gifts upon his anointed individuals, who play a crucial role in advancing the faith in the Lord Jesus Christ. The Lord grants gifts to those of his choosing, offering something special to every individual. It is essential to pray for and nurture these gifts so they can be used to serve the Lord God. These gifts have been instrumental in the writing of scriptures and the performance of numerous miracles

A man encountered the devil during his hospitalization in a mental institution. This hospitalization marked the onset of his exposure to the spiritual world, as he began to hear voices that seemed as real as a person speaking. Initially, he couldn't distinguish between good and evil; all voices sounded alike. Over time, however, he learned to discern and differentiate these voices.

Previous scriptures have documented the opening of eyes to the spiritual world. This teaching focuses on the opening of ears to the spiritual world.

A man heard a song sung by an evil spirit that had assailed him earlier that day. The spirit's song was the antithesis of what he later penned. It sang, "Even if you speak of Jesus, I will remain indifferent. I am content." Upon hearing this, he awoke, grabbed a book, and wrote a counter-song to challenge the devil, saying, "Even if you assail me for Jesus, I stand here content." Intriguingly, this malevolent spirit sang two distinct songs at separate times, which were combined to form the single song "Bona Obasinga" (greater than all). To the man, this song stands as one of the most potent ever composed, given its origin. The duration these spirits have sung this in the spiritual realm is unknown, but it is now a song they dread to hear sung by others—a composition of theirs that has turned into a weapon against them.

Voices are among the most challenging gifts one can encounter, yet they are the channels through which many scriptures have been written. The ability to discern these voices offers a deeper insight into the nature of evil. This concept has been the crux of my entire message. When God calls an individual, He imparts the wisdom to distinguish His voice from other spirits. This was one of the reasons He spent three years with His disciples; they learned His ways and character, enabling them to discern His voice from others. A man in a mental hospital, who was mistakenly believed to be insane, was actually overwhelmed by the voices he heard, unable to discern which to follow. What he valued in the mental hospital was the opportunity to listen and distinguish these voices. Although he never ceased to hear them, they became a constant in his life, guiding not the world at large, but his personal actions and destiny. Fortunately, he can now discern between the God and the devil.

When seated among friends or in a congregation, I can discern the source of communication. I assert again, 90% of your spoken and heard words are influenced by the spiritual world. Recognizing this, one ceases to condemn sinners. The actions deemed sinful are the character of the devil. The devil revels in the most corrupt dances imaginable, utters the most offensive vulgarity, and finds joy in deceit and sin. Upon encountering a drunkard, a member of the Homosexuality community, someone struggling with addiction to alcohol, sex, drugs, or someone who has committed violence, one should pray for their encounter with the Lord Jesus Christ. This book is penned for I know and understand the spiritual world I describe. Familiar with these malevolent spirits, I caution that they cannot be expelled by human means; only through divine intervention can such spirits and their influences be eradicated.

This is why I despise those who practice witchcraft and summon evil spirits beyond their comprehension. Can you recognize the appearance of the spirit of lust(fornication)? What these evil spirits do to man when you ask them to fail them getting married? You have asked them to kill him. Do you know how many of you have murdered unknowingly sending evil spirits to others? They will exert all their efforts to prevent him from obtaining what you have requested. He will resort to self-pleasure, become gay, and get HIV until he dies. For the evil spirit has fulfilled your request. Who is wed in death, and who gives birth in death?

Pray for the Lord God to reveal His gifts to you, for the world is in need of them. It is through these gifts that the Lord alerts humanity to the unseen spiritual realm. Cease fortifying the malevolent deeds of the devil. Pretending you were born gay is pretending you were born with sin and no one can separate you from that sin. God is perfect and makes no mistakes. However, the enemy seeks to undermine the good that the Lord has established. And you are made in the Lord's image. The devil will strive to destroy that divine beauty within you to satisfy his craving for sin.

# Lesson Sixty Five

# YOU ARE NOT A MISTAKE

The Lord Jesus Christ walked this earth and he knows all about the suffering you go through. He knew about you from the beginning and he knows well about your ending. That is the reason he came, for man to gain courage on this earth. For you to be strong and understand it's in the footsteps of your God that you walk on this earth.

It's hard to fathom the emotions felt by the disciples when the Lord Jesus Christ was departing from them. Reading His words to the disciples, one can sense the profound sadness among the eleven who had been with Him for the past three years. He was about to leave them, never to be seen again in this earthly life.

In the Book of John, the Lord Jesus Christ fortifies the disciples by recognizing that He has traversed this earth Himself. He comprehends the tribulations His children endure. He encourages you to remain steadfast and be aware that He is always with you. The Lord Jesus Christ has journeyed through this world and He empathizes with you deeply. One of the most significant assurances I can offer you is that God will never assign you a task beyond your capacity to manage.

All are created by God, who knows precisely what each can bear. Considering Moses's character, would he have been a better Abraham, known as a humble, obedient servant of God? Could Paul have been a good Moses, one who respects his leadership role and remains steadfast with his people until the end?

You are not a mistake; your path in Christ is purposeful. The Lord God recognizes that you are better suited than those before you to embark on this journey. Consider the man admitted to a mental hospital, struggling with voices from the spiritual realm he initially couldn't distinguish. Over time, he began to discern them. One of the most startling revelations he received from the devil was this: While the Lord Jesus Christ fasted in the wilderness for 40 days, as documented in Luke's scriptures, all the fallen angels were present in that desert. The devil purportedly questioned the Lord, "Why did you cast us out of heaven?"

When the Bible discusses the temptation of Jesus Christ, it is often perceived that there is only one tempter: the devil. However, this 'devil' symbolizes a collective representation of numerous others. Jesus faced more temptations than what is documented in the scriptures. The plea in the Lord's Prayer in Matthew, 'lead us not  into temptation,' acknowledges the frailty of mankind in the face of temptation.

The man in the mental hospital endured a difficult journey for years. He had a feeling that perhaps in one month, the voices would cease. But this was part of his calling. It is the reason these scriptures are being written. For many prophets and apostles never wrote these words. It is the reason we speak what many couldn't speak, for where they come from not everyone will be there. Don't believe Moses slept and woke up to write. He possessed the spiritual ears to hear the Lord's voice, just as one person listens to another.  It was his true calling, and as the most suitable man for the task, he achieved success.  Be strong in your calling. You're not here to enjoy this earth like the earthly descendants. You are God's child and part of God's mission to save man from sin. Your reward is in heaven. Once this has passed, your experiences will become a hymn to your past.

I urge you to persevere. It's only a matter of days before you enter the Lord's presence. He traversed this earth and is familiar with its trials. He understands how the devil has marred His cherished creation. By surrendering to Him and following His path, He will guide you. Ward off the devil by invoking the Holy Spirit . Just as the Lord Jesus Christ triumphed over His terrestrial struggles, the Holy Spirit will fortify and safeguard you until He brings you to the Father.

# Lesson Sixty Six

## LISTEN TO GOD'S VOICE, HE SPEAKS

Being in a state of sin may hinder your ability to hear God's voice. Nevertheless, God persists in speaking and reaching out to you. If you take a moment to pause, you can hear His voice distinctly, for He speaks in a way that is audible to you. When you liberate yourself from sin, you will realize the clarity with which His voice echoes.

One cannot comprehend how God cares for His people, nor will one ever understand. Neither on this earth nor in heaven. His power and might are unparalleled by any being. All that is necessary to know is that He is present, and His gaze is upon His people every second.

In the Book of Job, God inquires of satan, "Where have you come from?" satan answers, "From roaming throughout the earth, and walking back and forth on it." It's not that the Lord was unaware of satan's whereabouts. Rather, God's reminder to the devil is that nothing can be done beyond His watchful presence.

Consider yourself, a man marked by sin, walking the earth with indifference to the life you lead. It is undeniable how comfortable humanity has grown on this planet. Do you choose to commit acts of violence under the belief that you are unseen?

Yet a voice beckons, asking, 'Where are you, my child?' The Lord urges you to flee from the sin that approaches. The Lord Jesus teaches that when a spirit encounters an unoccupied soul, it summons seven others more unclean than itself. However, the Lord perpetually invites His children to draw near to Him. You perceive these calls, yet you choose the sinful path offered by the devil.

As a married woman, you may find yourself facing the advances of a younger colleague whose intentions are solely to engage in a physical relationship. At 32 years of age, with a husband and child, you may experience inner turmoil when deciding whether to entertain this proposition. Should you allow yourself to entertain the idea, the allure of this individual could potentially sway your judgment. Trust me, God is reaching out to you, saying, "I see the devil nearby, come closer to me. Here with me, there is no sin." The voice is present; God is beckoning. If she listens to this voice, she will find salvation. Yet, many choose to heed a different voice that conjures false illusions in their minds. You must listen, truly listen. The Lord speaks and calls out. Once you hear His voice, all other voices become insignificant. Just listen.

# Lesson Sixty Seven

# WE WERE CREATED WITH LOVE

God created all things the most beautiful and that includes you, man. However, by embracing sin, that inherent beauty created by God has been tarnished within you. Consider the wealthy; they have all they need but don't look loved. This is because sin has eroded and destroyed the Godly love that was created in them.

A man fell asleep and had a vision. He saw a homeless man who had passed away on the street, a beggar. He appeared filthy and unclean, his face unrecognizable. In that same dream, the man's life after death was revealed. In the after life, the beggar was transformed into the most beautiful person he had ever seen, with a radiance and shades of skin unlike any he had witnessed on earth.

Upon awakening from his dream, he understood that everyone was crafted with love. God fashioned you in love, and it is you who have strayed from that love. Whether sinners or not, you are His creation, made with the most profound gift He possesses—love.

On this earth, hate is personified by those who walk in the soiled garments of sin. Sin has inflicted pain upon the children of flesh, enslaving them. Even those with abundant wealth are not spared from this pain, for they too walk in the realm of sin. Their riches cannot buy them love.

The sole source of love is the giver of love, who bestows his gifts upon his children. He commanded the angels, "Take off those dirty clothes." You must strive to seek your creator's love, for neglecting him has allowed the world to dictate your identity. The pursuit of material possessions will never grant you the peace and love he offers. It is a profound honor to dedicate your life to finding the love of your God, for he is not concealed; all who seek him shall find him. In finding him, you will experience his love and joy, which the world cannot strip from you.